What People are Saying About Year 13...

TJ Greaney shares his powerful story in this book and shows how God can redeem our broken lives for our good and His glory. Now TJ's passion for training men to disciple young boys is fueled by a tender heart that was once broken himself as a young man. Check out his story and also the cool ministry of Kids Outdoor Zone.

Stephen Kendrick, Filmmaker, *Overcomer, War Room, Courageous, Fireproof, Facing the Giants*

I first met TJ at a men's conference in Kalispell, Montana, where we both served as speakers. That event led to a lunch together where we found we shared similar passions for helping boys become men. But what really connected me to TJ was his BIG HEART for helping fatherless boys find themselves and the love of God alongside male mentors in the outdoors. What a priceless gift to these young men! I only wish I could clone a thousand TJ's.

TJ's passion, like mine, didn't just happen. God providentially crafted both our drives out of a challenging upbringing and painful struggle.

Pain that was graciously forged into gain; bad into a greater good. Year 13 *lets you peer into TJ's life journey. It will encourage and inspire you, I promise. I highly recommend it.*

Dr. Robert Lewis, Founder, Men's Fraternity, and author of *Raising a Modern-Day Knight*

YEAR 13

A wounded boy's
journey to
manhood
and ministry

YEAR 13

A wounded boy's journey to manhood and ministry

T. J. GREANEY

Founder of KOZ: Kids Outdoor Zone

KOZ PUBLISHING COMPANY
Austin, Texas

Photo Credit: Jon-Michael Greaney, TJ Greaney

Book Design: TLC Graphics, *TLCGraphics.com*
Cover: Tamara Dever, Interior: Erin Stark

ISBN: 978-0-9909924-2-4
ISBN: 978-0-9909924-3-1 (Audiobook)
ISBN: 978-0-9909924-4-8 (E-book)

First Edition

Printed in the United States

Jesus, thank you for the rescue.

To my wife Sandra,
you make this whole adventure worthwhile.

To Cody, Nicole, Saylor, Taylor, and Jon-Michael.
I could not be more proud of you.
Remember, nothing good happens after midnight,
do hard things, and follow the King.

HIKERS TO GRAYSON
IGHLANDS STATE PARK:
OLLOW APPALACHIAN TR.
(WHITE BLAZES)

Table of Contents

Introduction

Life is a collection of memories. They come and go as your heart is moved. Sadness, anger, joy, and laughter all bring back thoughts from yesterday, last month, a year ago, or even many years ago. There are so many. A smell, a sound, a song, or a landscape can trigger them from the very deepest places that once seemed forgotten or packed away—things lost in the recesses of the mind that find their way out. It can be incredibly enlightening, incredibly painful, or just reflective.

I know some people have terrible repressed memories. Wounds so deep, so horrible, and so scary that to even consider allowing them into our minds can cause us to tremble. For some, they have worked through the wounds in counseling, or Christ has brought them peace through His grace and love. Some have learned to live with the past, learned to accept the sins of their transgressions. Some of us have just put things so deep we don't think we will ever have to deal with them again. Good riddance. What many of us don't realize is that these things have formed us in every way.

I think a lot about the legacy I will leave behind. I so dearly want to leave a long trail of memories that bring a joyful reflection. My dear friend Lee died way too soon. One day, he was bugging me and trying to order a wife from Russia, the next he was calling me from his hospital bed. It seemed so sudden and then such a short time before Hospice pulled the sheets over him.

Lee had a lot of ideas and thoughts. He was a true idea man. One thing Lee always talked about was how when the clock showed 11:11, he was hearing from God or something special was supposed to happen. 11:11 was his personal time. Lee's 11:11 thing has kept his memory, his legacy, his funny little way of laughing, and his presence alive. I say hi to him every time I see it, and I see it a lot. I am very enamored by the whole effect 11:11 has had on my wife and me.

In the book *The Road Less Traveled,* author Scott Peck opens with "Life is difficult." Yep, it sure is. It is hard, and lots of things go wrong. People do things to us and let us down, and we get deep, deep wounds and hurts. Sometimes we wonder if we will ever see the light—if we will ever get relief from the seemingly endless pains and hardships. Why me, why not them? We blame God. How could You let this happen? I just want to be left alone, pain-free.

John Eldredge at Ransomed Heart Ministries talks about "Agreements." These are the wounds and sins we accept as a part of who we are. We "Agree," assisted by satan's promptings and influence, to believe untrue things about ourselves. To me—the school dropout, the drug using street kid was who I was. I spent years as a callused head-down worker with dreams and desires that rarely became real. My heart so dearly desired meaning, family, and the search for my true self. Deep inside I wanted to be something, but I did not understand what. I was driven but not always by the right things.

The wounds and victories in these pages are the things that trained me for His work. Each of us has been trained or is in training for Kingdom work. How does it all fit? How can those terrible things I did yesterday, this morning, or that happened to me as a child have anything to do with a loving heavenly Father?

A friend of mine posted on his Facebook not long ago that he always wanted to go to the post office with his grandfather because he would always find money. Now, he didn't particularly want to go anywhere with his grandfather, but he loved the trip to the post office every day because of the random coins he would find there. It was a treasure hunt, an adventure with a reward. Looking back now, reflecting on those drives with his grandfather, he covets the time they spent together. He found out later the coins were not random but placed by his grandfather to create those memories. Intentional, thought out, planned. I can picture his grandfather smiling as he placed the coins and watched his little grandson explore and discover the treasure. Joy. His grandfather participated in his legacy—that is wisdom. We do not usually see or understand God's plan as He rolls it out.

This is my story. This is how God took that broken street kid and used him for His purposes. I don't claim any special gifts or prideful works I did to find what He has for me. It was all Him, Jesus Christ, Father God, and the Holy Spirit. He chose me. I do my best to follow and stay in His presence. I don't want to claim it to be in any way perfect either because I can assure you it is not. What I can promise is this life, living for Jesus, is the closest thing to knowing my heart and my feelings than anything I have ever done. It has given me purpose in a battle that I longed for. If you choose to ride this trail with Him, hold on, it will be an amazing ride.

1

Indigo

Living in Houston as a young boy were good days. Dad had served his time in the military, and one benefit after he was out was the ability to purchase our home at 5901 Indigo. A small GI home in a neighborhood full of quaint little GI homes of the same size and style. I remember the floors were all hardwood. There was a small living room, kitchen, and a long hall with three bedrooms. The room at the end was my parents' master bedroom. They had the one window air conditioner unit in their bedroom, and we relished it on hot days. The kitchen and living room were the gathering place when we were inside. I remember sitting at the dinner table together each night. The Catholic dinner prayer and manners were expected.

Our little family filled the house to capacity. There are five of us kids. The oldest is John, I am second, then in order, Cathy, Mike, and Gen. Again, we were a standard-issue Catholic family. I spent a lot more time with my older brother. Most guys want to follow their big brother around. The younger ones spent a lot of time together too. Life happened in our little house there on Indigo.

The proximity to the Gulf Coast made beach runs easy. We spent lots of time on the beach in Galveston, Texas, learning to swim, sunning, and relaxing. Mom tells of how she would look up, count five heads, and then go back to what she was doing. She was always counting to make sure one of us didn't get swept away.

Dad always had us trying to catch crabs. He would put out wooden stakes and tie a string with a chicken leg or neck to one end. Big blue crabs as fresh as they come were plentiful, and we would take turns trying to net them.

If you live by the Gulf of Mexico long enough, you will experience hurricanes. Hurricane Carla slammed into the coast just south of Houston in September of 1963; I was four years old. Carla ranks as the most intense tropical cyclone to make landfall by the National Weather Service's Hurricane Severity Index. Damage was widespread. I remember that during the eye of the storm, Mom and Dad let us out on the front porch. Branches, dead birds, roof shingles, and other debris were in the yard. We played with our full-size metal Tonka trucks as the gray sky swirled overhead. I can still see it now looking up at the sky—a blue hole with angry, gray clouds circling around it.

As the wind and rain returned, our parents ushered us back into the house. The wind-force pushed the rain through the windows, and Mom had towels rolled up against the sills. I wasn't afraid in that storm, in that house, or with my family.

In Houston, the yard was our playground, the trees our adventure towers, and most of my memories happened outside. The chinaberry tree in the backyard was a very important element. I don't know if that is the technical biological name or not, but the berries grew hard in the spring and were perfect for throwing and slingshots. The tree grew tall, and we used it to build all types of forts, perches, and lookouts. Every boy needs a tree, and that was mine.

So many days I remember climbing as high as I could get and peering out into the front yard and the backyards around us with the warm, moist breeze on my face. We sat under the shade of its big branches in the heat of the summers. We never complained about wanting to go inside to lay around and watch one of the three channels on our television.

One day we found a small sparrow that had fallen from its nest. We took him in, named him Chirpy, and cared for him. Every morning Chirpy would wake up and hop down the hall into the kitchen chirping. The memory brings a joyful feeling to my heart, so I have to believe there was joy there. Then, one night John insisted on Chirpy sleeping with him in his bed. Mom was against it but gave in. Sometime in the night he must have rolled over on Chirpy and smothered him. I remember Mom or Dad saying, "I told you so," and that was it. I think it was the first time I ever had to deal with death on a personal level—death of something I loved and cared for. The memory stops there.

Dad was an incredible carpenter. He built us a playhouse back in the corner of our backyard. It was a small replica of our home with rafters, windows, wood siding, and a door. This was a place I look back and wonder about. It was a place I made choices that I am not sure where they came from. I had to be in single digit age, and I wasn't influenced by anything you might consider a bad influence—no porn magazines, no internet, and no TV. Maybe the things that happened were just a boy being a boy.

One kid on the block ended up there in our playhouse one day with a fresh cut on his finger. He was in a panic mode to make it go away, so I came up with what I told him was a classic cure for a cut by every doctor. I ran in the house and got salt. I poured it on the cut and immediately things got worse. I told him not to worry, that was supposed to happen. The next step was to rinse it off in the water still standing out along the front curb. Dead earthworms and dirt particles were all part of the healing elixir. It did not seem to help his pain, and he ran off home. I don't remember ever playing with that kid again.

A little girl my age lived across the street, and at some point, I lured her into the playhouse. Of course, I was a doctor; I think I mentioned that, didn't I? I suggested I check her for any diseases or other infirmities she might have and not know about. She didn't go for it. Thinking back now, she might have been that other boy's kid sister. My medical skills may have come into question.

Then there was the day I was exploring the playhouse construction with its solid 2 x 4 wall framing with tight corners, perfectly aligned and measured. Climbing around in the upper levels, I could see the impeccable 2 x 6 angle cuts of the rafters my dad had crafted to fit against the ridge beam. Plywood and shingle covered the rafters and kept out every drop of rain.

While I was up there that day, I had a random thought. What would happen if I held a match to the bare wood on one rafter? I took out a match, lit it, and held it there. Where the heck I got a wooden strike match anywhere, I do not know. The dry 2 x 6 burned easily. I stared and watched it as it crept up the light-colored pine wood. The flame bright, leaving a red and black trail. Then I snapped out of it. Wait, what did I do? The fire was getting too big; I couldn't blow it out. I climbed down and ran for the only water source I could think of, the dog bowl. I ran back and threw it up into the ceiling. The fire grew.

I ran into the house and told Mom. She went into action and called the fire department, then worked on getting the hose out during the chaos and confusion.

I can feel the emotion of disappointment in myself today as I write this. I don't know where the matches came from. I can't explain why I did what I did; I just can't. Mom asked me right before she spanked me why I did it, and I had no answer. Dad tore the charred and burned remains down. That was it for the playhouse. All his hard work, money, and craftsmanship destroyed in one strike of a wooden kitchen match. I have a sense of shame and disappointment that I did that and hurt my dad. I also do not remember him reacting to it—no whipping, no scolding, and no beatings. I don't understand why not. I deserved a butt whipping for sure.

The front yard area, the neighborhood, and the blocks around was a land of adventure in itself, and we explored every inch. The tall grass that grew up against the house always hid small grass snakes we would collect. Slugs, crickets, and green lizards were plentiful and always stopped us for a curious thought. The slugs usually required salt, the lizards lost tails as we tried to catch them, but if we did, crickets were force-fed treats for them. The bushes had yellow-jacket wasps that would sting us if we were not careful. We knew every inch of the yard.

The street in front was a quiet neighborhood street that on most any given day would be full of kids on bikes riding up and down. One day I had discovered a mud puddle; it was just the perfect consistency to make mud pies, mud cakes, and mud bombs. Somehow I found myself as the aggressor, and as kids rode by on their bikes, I threw the perfectly formed mud bombs at them. It had to be a game they enjoyed because I remember they kept riding by. At one point, I threw the perfect gooey brown bomb, and it missed its target. I couldn't stand to see a good blob of mud go to waste, so I ran out into the street to retrieve it.

Wham. I was crushed by a biker, and my head was slashed open. Blood flowed freely down my face as I ran into the house for Mom. Stitches were required. Again, "Why did you do that?" and again, "I don't know." Two things I surmise from this ordeal. One is that the little boy I doctored on earlier may have been the culprit who ran over my face. An unhappy patient? Secondly, as a parent today, I think the parents of the kids around our house probably thought we were the rough kids and tried to keep their kids at a distance.

Our garage was the workshop, and Dad used it that way. One of the coolest DIY (Do It Yourself) projects he built would be a smashing success on Pinterest today. He built a drawer storage unit from used cigar boxes. He took about twenty of the same King Edward cigar boxes, removed the tops, and put small wooden pulls on the fronts. He built a wooden cabinet for them to fit into, stackable. In those little treasure boxes, you could find just about everything cool, like screws, nuts, small tools, and other mechanical pieces. Every time you opened one, it was a surprise.

Of course, Dad might not have been super happy that we would pilfer his organized drawers, and I would guess we were not near as concerned about where things were returned. But that was a cool storage container built for a boy's wandering mind.

Then there was the time Dad decided to build a go-cart. Oh, yes, yes, yes. He took an old wagon, a gas edger motor, and other sprockets and bolts. He built it from scratch. On the day of its christening, Dad let John be the driver. Dad started the motor and released the back of our racing wagon. John took off. He rolled down the driveway, turned to the right onto Indigo then just as he got to where our yard ended, it died. It never ran again.

The failure of the handmade go-cart spawned the motor era at our house. Dad bought us a Sears minibike. We rode that thing everywhere. What more could a boy ask for? It had fat tires, a fast motor, could take a beating, and made us extra cool in the neighborhood—at least with the kids.

The minibike went great until the day I was riding on the back as my older brother swept down the neighborhood streets and a cop pulled us over. What, after all this time? He wrote us a list of tickets. Dad was mad. How could a store sell a minibike that we could not use on the street in our little neighborhood? How come now, after all these months of us terrorizing the streets, yards, backyards, and parks around there could this happen? The judge said it was not street legal; the minibike days ended there.

Thank goodness Dad still had the failed go-cart on his mind because one day as we were driving down our street, we saw the most incredible site—a low-profile racing go-cart half out of a neighbor's garage. It was awesome. Incredibly, Dad stopped, backed up, and got out. So did my brother and I. Dad talked with the man as John and I dreamed of racing the beast. Dad bought it. Wow!

We would take the low-profile cart to the mall parking lot on Sunday afternoons. The stores in those days were closed on Sundays, and the wide-open expanse of pavement was perfect. That cart was so fast, scary fast. It wasn't long before we learned to run it wide open. I loved the smell of the gas and oil mixture burning in light blue smoke, the oil stains on our clothes, and the high-pitched whine of the motor. It was an incredible time. Then one day, the cart shut down. Dad couldn't get it to run again. As quickly as they began, the racing cart days were over. But for the kids on Indigo, for us, the adventures continued.

2

A BB Gun
and the Bayou

Why my dad trusted us with BB guns, I can't say for sure. I can just say he was cool that way. We had Red Ryders from early on. I heard a saying once that seems to fit here. It was, "Give a boy a hammer, and everything looks like a nail." For a boy with a Red Ryder, every object fixed or fragile was a target. Nothing alive was safe in our hunting area inside the backyard. It was the original game-fenced ranch. I think our favorite hunts would be the sparrow hunts. We launched thousands and thousands of copper BB's from our trusted rifles at the small brown-feathered birds that made the mistake of landing in our tree, on the electric lines, or atop the chain link fence.

Dad had laid a back patio made of brick. He graded the soil, laid a layer of sand, and then meticulously set red brick in lines. Between each brick was more sand. Around the outside of the brick patio floor, he built flower beds and a huge barbeque smoker and grill all by hand, all perfectly crafted. He was good.

John and I were standing on the brick flower beds one sunny afternoon. My sister, Cathy, was there too. Somehow my brother talked me into taking a shot from his BB gun to the stomach. He put the gun right up against the skin and pop. The sting was excruciating. All agreements were off. "Mom, Mom, John just shot me." I think we lost our guns for a while.

Back then, John Wayne was a role model for every boy, and the movie *Hatari* was a favorite of my older brother, myself, and our friends. In the 1967 movie, Wayne was an animal trapper on the plains of Africa and could catch anything. His pole and rope loop snare was all he needed to face off and cage even the most brutal rhinoceros. We designed a similar one from willow branches and cotton twine. We worked the waterways, ditches, and buoys around the house for hours, days, and months.

Houston is known as the Bayou City. The bayou was just at the end of the street, and for us, it was an incredible place for adventure, danger, and exploration. There were the hard-sided concrete ones that took huge amounts of water to the gulf, and the smaller ones that fed into them that had cattails, rocks, sand, and willows. Wildlife was abundant. Snakes, turtles, and frogs were everywhere.

Snakes—mostly poisonous, black water moccasins—were our primary target. One day we caught several really large ones and thought up the idea to sell them to the Houston Zoo. It was brilliant; they would appreciate our skills and surely give us cash. Actually, they freaked out. They told our mom what we had, and she freaked out. At that point, we were forced to let them go back at the bayou.

My best friend was Roy Newman. Roy lived right next door, and we did everything together. Roy was missing a half finger on one hand. It was my first real experience with a difference in a person physically, but it was cool. We explored every corner of the neighborhood as growing boys.

We were together on a bayou run when my brother caught a huge snapping turtle. He told me to hold it while we continued to hunt. I struggled to keep him from pushing away, and his claws dug into my arms. I moved him close to my face taunting him and bragged how he was mine and not going anywhere. That is when he struck. The snapping turtle is known for its fast strike to catch its food. He was mad and clamped down with a death grip on my chin. I, of course, freaked out, and my brother said, "Don't freak out." He smacked, slapped, pulled, and prodded, to no avail. Finally, the beast let go, and I threw him on the bank. My mom must have been exasperated when she heard the story and doctored my chin. Boys, ugh. It didn't deter me for long. I was a boy, and the scar was just another story.

During the summers, we took the American vacations as a family. Dad built a trailer that held all our gear. It had pockets, drawers, and cubbies for all Mom's cooking gear, the tent, chairs, and lantern. This was the ultimate camper trailer, and I am guessing Dad had a lot of folks asking him about it when we traveled. We did the whole camping thing right. I found the list Mom wrote way back then that included every item she needed to pack before a trip. It had penciled in notes, check marks, and fit inside a Shell Gas brochure during car camping. Back in those days, gas stations pumped your gas, gave away free maps, and other cool things like "how to" brochures on all kinds of car adventuring.

One warm weekend, we had gone to Huntsville State Park just north of Houston. The park had a beautiful little lake and a small floating marina. I don't remember getting the shiny Zebco fishing pole, but I had one. I got worms at the marina store, found a spot on the dock away from all the commotion, and started fishing. My fishing memories start here. I must have had some knowledge because I sat with a bobber, hooking on my own worms.

There was one moment I can visualize to this day. I hooked on a worm and dropped it in. Wham! It was a fish—a huge fish—a sun perch as big as my hand. The adrenaline and excitement were so powerful. To this day, I claim that fish as my first fish. My hands were probably not that big to think of it now, but in my mind, my world, that was huge, and something inside registered with it. I loved fishing.

The national parks were and are incredible—Yellowstone, Grand Canyon, Grand Teton, Sequoia, Glacier, Great Sand Dunes, and so many more. We traveled through New Mexico, California, Colorado, Wyoming, and Texas. We saw so much. Mom cooked with camping gear. The tent was a big canvas three-room job, and we split big kids, little kids, and Mom and Dad into each section.

There are so many memories of outdoor adventure and awe. One evening, as we sat at our mountainside campsite watching the weather below, the clouds rolling across the valley formed a tornado and touched down. All the adults stood watching the twister picking up hay and small brush and throwing it around. I freaked out. I was asking my mom and dad, what do we do, is it coming up here, how are you going to protect us? That was when I learned you lie down in the ditch, and it goes right over the top of you. I didn't feel much better about the whole thing when they told me that is what I should do. I was scared that day. That may explain my gut reaction every time I see the tornado scene in the *Wizard of Oz*.

Another night on that trip, we woke to squealing, loud chirping, and growling noises outside the tent. Then there was a colliding sound against the side of our tent and another loud growl. In the morning, we woke to find small chipmunk tracks up and over our tent, as well as two large bear paw prints with claw holes just above where I was sleeping. I was ready to leave that particular campground.

On the way home, we were blessed to enjoy one of the rare Holiday Inn stops. The big night included take-out food in the room. The room had good beds for jumping and a quarter vibrating machine on each. That night we fell asleep happy and tired only to be awakened in the middle of the night in confusion. The room was dark and blurry as I tried to figure out what was going on. Mom was mad at Dad, and he was stumbling around the room. He had just come in, and something was wrong with him.

This is my first memory of my dad being drunk. At the time we never knew what really happened and I was not going to ask. Mom and Dad protected us from what was going on in their relationship and his drinking. Somewhere along the way, I heard Dad had gone out drinking; some girl had slipped him a "mickey" and stolen his wallet. We made it home. That was when the long camping trips and family vacations with Dad ended.

Catholic Church and School

During our time on Indigo, Mom and Dad hosted a lot of foster kids, all teenage girls. They were not with us too long, but a couple stayed long enough to make an impression. They became a part of our family and did everything we did. We never thought anything different about them; they were just family for that season.

We went to a Catholic church and school when we were on Indigo Street. I made my way through all the lesson plans and ceremonial levels of being a good Catholic boy. I don't downplay the things I learned; I just know my heart was never engaged. Those things were just what you did.

Confession was a regular event back then; we had to do it as part of our weekly school schedule. I had a system down, a spiel. I always included a few times I punched my sister, said bad words, and disobeyed my mom. They weren't actual events; they just got my turn in front of the little curtain-covered window over. It must have been excruciating to be the priest listening to all those kids each week. I doubt I was the only boy who made up a good list of bad things to be forgiven for. I bet they drew straws or the newest priest at the church had to do the school confessions.

I was in second or third grade when I found myself sitting in class alone. I was close to the front, maybe row three or four and center. Why I was the only one in class makes no sense. I guess being such a stellar young man, they let me roam about unhindered.

Everyone had left out one textbook on their desks. I was sitting at my desk, took my pencil, turned around, and picked up the textbook that belonged to the boy sitting behind me. I scribbled and marked the whole outside of it scratching and leaving dark pencil marks on the binding and page edges. Then I put it back on his desk.

When the class returned, of course, he saw the vandalized book and told Sister Maria. As we all sat in horror, she asked the class who did it. Confess. I was the first to chime in with "It wasn't me." The questioning stopped there, and I was ushered to the front of the room. "Why did you do that, Thomas?" "I didn't do it." She asked the question again. Finally, I answered, "I don't know."

That was when she took out a ruler and swatted my hands. I was humiliated. Yes, I did the dastardly deed; why, because that kid irritated me is all I can think of. I remember feeling humiliated and angry about her doing that. It was classic Nun punishment.

My Sports Career

Baseball was my sport. My brother played, and so did I. We played on the local public teams, and I loved it. I was actually pretty good. Part of my youth picture collection includes a series of team pictures, and I can vaguely remember something about all the teams. I played all areas of the field. My favorite was the infield. Second base and shortstop were my spots. I also became a really reliable hitter. My eye-hand coordination was tight, and every time I got up to bat I connected with the ball. My coaches praised me, and my place on the team was important.

Then came the slump. I fumbled and lost my confidence. I don't know what happened. Was it something at home that had me upset? Was it Mother Nature? I don't know, but our team was kicking tail and went into the playoffs with me sitting on the bench.

One night as a playoff game ended and I helped pack the gear, my dad approached the coach. I had been on the bench the whole game. By now I had figured out Dad drank, and sometimes it caused problems. I knew Dad had been drinking that night, probably while sitting in the car. He read the riot act to the coach for not putting me into the game. I knew he was intoxicated, but it was my dad taking up for me. It wasn't right that Coach did not let me play; every kid should play. Dad made sure he knew that. I was embarrassed that my drunk father was there, but I was so glad he was there for me and stood up for me. Drunk or not, it was something. To this day, I remember it and consider it a good thing. Is that weird? Not for a boy.

The next year I got my confidence back, and I was a beast on the field. I was the coach's favorite. I could hit, field, and do it all, and the coach praised me like never before. I was soaring. Then, in the middle of the season, we moved. I remember we talked about how I would get back and forth, the long drives, the time. It was not going to work, so I transferred to an existing team in our new town. I was no longer the beast. I was the outsider, the new guy, the kid who would take someone else's spot. My game was off, and it never came back. Baseball was done.

My youngest years were so transformative to who I would be, what my heart longs for, and loves. For the most part, the family functioned as a family. We did things together. We saw amazing things and learned more than I knew. I was at a good age to experience all of the trips and time as a family together. I did not realize there was more going on between Mom and Dad and that life as I knew it was about to change.

3

Clear Lake

I was in the fourth grade when we moved. Dad had worked with Shell Oil Company for years when he got the job offer with a small company south of Houston. The job must have been a good one. We rented a house while Mom and Dad built the custom home of their dreams in the influential neighborhood of Nassau Bay, Texas. While we were waiting for the house, I went to the local elementary school.

At the time, I was a pretty sharp dresser. I had just come from a private school with uniforms so I must have been in a pretty weird place. I remember one particular fashion statement I made. I had a "dickey" I wore to school all the time. If you don't know what a dickey is, think a turtleneck with flaps—a fake turtleneck. Fashion can be a brutal mistress, and being a trendsetter is hard for an elementary grade boy—especially one with the super large ears, big nose, and general goofy look of my face. I thought about that every day when I looked in the mirror, horrified. But I had my dickey and somehow, some way, that made things better.

The rental house was on the corner of a cul-de-sac. The backyard was small, long, and narrow. This was a builder's neighborhood without any real trees. Maybe some small ones had been planted in recent years, but nothing like where we had come from. Shade was hard to find unless it was inside.

We met other kids in the "hood." Two guys my older brother's age were at the back of the street—Craig and his brother Bobby. They were stepbrothers, and that was the first time I ever thought about split families or step-families. I don't remember ever seeing a dad. Just them and their mom.

Craig was a handsome guy with a square cut chin and fit. He was a star football player and had the swagger of a good high school athlete who knew he was good-looking and an important man on campus. Bobby, on the other hand, was a bit heavy and not quite as confident, but he was more cocky than secure. I am guessing he rode the coattails of his step-brother. Together they were a force to reckon with, and I liked them. Craig, in a lot of ways, was everything I wanted to be, and his brother was everything I felt.

Life changed for me after the move. It was a mixture of my age and the lack of stability and security I had grown up with. I can still feel the change in my heart and spirit that began to happen.

One day, I found myself hanging out at Craig and Bobby's house. To be invited into their world was a big deal. For the most part, I usually just sat and absorbed their wisdom, opinions, and ideas. I remember that day I kept looking up at the ceiling over their beds. Hanging in long strands were yellow, brown, and off-white blobs of different sizes and lengths. Some were more splattered than others.

In a squeaky voice, not wanting to be noticed, I asked what was hanging from the ceiling over their beds. The brothers looked at each other and laughed. "Those are loogies. We have contests who can spit one up there, get it to stick, and hang down the farthest." They laughed at my reaction. I wanted to barf. To this day, as I write this, I am on the verge of puking. That had to be one of the grossest things ever. How could they do that and not throw up? How could their mom let them do that? How could they get them up that high and get them to stick?

I also think this was when I first heard about pot. These guys alluded to it, hinted about it. I clued in and started listening very intently to their conversations. These guys really smoked marijuana? They weren't hippies or murderers. They were football players, guys on our street, regular guys in my world. My world was changing fast.

The little rental house had a detached garage, and one hot summer day I was exploring the rafters and some boxes left up there from the previous renters. I was digging through them not finding much of anything except near the end, in a smaller box inside a box, inside another box. The smallest box was unusually heavy.

As I unfolded the flaps, I saw a semi-round dark green, black, and silver ball. No, it wasn't a ball; it was pineapple-shaped. Holy crap, it was a hand grenade. A real live, pin inside, never used, ready-to-explode hand grenade. I held that thing, looking at it, thinking about that pin, what I should do, and what I could do. I got down from the rafters with my newfound gem in hand and took it inside and showed Mom. Oh my gosh, she went crazy. She had me put it back in the garage and come inside the house. She immediately called the sheriff's office.

When the sheriff arrived, he asked Mom a lot of questions. Who lived there before us, did we know it was there, were there any more? Then he carefully carried it, placed it inside his trunk, and drove away. I guess he took it to the place where hand grenades went to back then. I'm guessing the sheriff survived. You know, today they would have had a robot and the bomb squad out, and we would have been evacuated. If I found one today, that thing would go straight to the ranch, and the pin pulled and chunked. (For liability reasons, I have to say "Not really." But you decide what you think.)

There was a lot of science going on at that time. I remember back then breaking thermometers on purpose and playing with the silver liquid in our hands, on the table, and eventually losing it all somehow. Somewhere. I loved taking electrical things apart and putting them back together. The now-defunct electronic store Radio Shack was a heavenly place. Dad would take us there and buy do-it-yourself radio kits, switches, wires, and other cool stuff. I would spend hours in my room making things from electric motors and wires, flashlight bulbs, and old radios. I was not very smart. I did not invent the first computer or the atomic bomb. However, I did learn a few things.

Somehow along the way, I think Mom noticed my brother and I were being influenced by the new lifestyle we were immersed in. A mom's intuition is almost always right. She must have had a feeling a change was happening, and we needed to be shown something important we would not forget that would cause us to feel slightly guilty about how blessed we were.

One Sunday, Mom loaded John and me up in the car. We had no idea where she was taking us, but it was just he and I, and she was not to be argued with.

We were never disrespectful to my parents in any way. Not while I was little. We grew up with "yes sir" and "yes ma'am." Dad had been in the Marines and both my parents grew up in pretty strict homes, so there were no "yea" or "uh-huh" answers. We were kids and acted as kids do, but we knew when to get in the car, do our chores, and not argue.

She drove us down and around, and finally she turned off the highway. Ahead of us was a long winding driveway that led atop a hill where a large white house stood. There were long columns at the front declaring the colonial style which was typical for the area. We parked in a designated area off to the side of the home. The parking area was a mixture of gravel and oyster shell. There was a sign out front that read "Boys Town" (not sure this is an accurate name).

What the heck was a Boys Town? This could be cool, a place for us to have fun, hang out. Mom ushered us out of the car and to the front door where we were met by a friendly woman. She was expecting Mom. She told us about the home and what they did. She was focused on John and me as she described the living conditions and the order of the days for the boys. Oh, yes, boys only.

Finally, we were ushered into a large dining room. We sat at a table, and in came a bunch of boys. There were other adults at other tables. Family, friends, aunts, uncles, and grandparents, I suppose. The lady who had been telling us about the home brought over some boys. Sitting with them was very awkward. They asked us questions about who we were, where we lived, and whether we had a mom and dad. They had done this before, but they seemed genuinely interested.

We found out they had been dropped off there by their parents, or they didn't know their parents. They didn't go home at the end of the day, or week, or month. They lived here in this big white house with worn wood siding and cavernous rooms. They ate together and slept in bunk beds lined against the walls in each dorm room. They showered in a big bathroom with multiple showers, open, all together.

I liked them, but I didn't understand what happened to them. I was exposed to kids living in a divorce or split family with Craig and Bobby—now this. Kids without families?

At that moment, on that Sunday afternoon, somewhere inside me I felt sadness, compassion, loneliness for these boys. I don't think we ever knew why Mom took us there. Maybe to be taught to appreciate what we had, or maybe to see what happens to boys who don't mind their parents. Probably both. Maybe Mom was questioning if she could keep us all together and, if she was forced to disband our family, how her boys would weather the storm in a boy's home.

One thing for sure, on that day, something registered with me and a seed was planted deep, deep inside. Years later, Mom told me that on the way home, I said, "One day I am going to build a ranch where boys who don't have a family can come."

4

Nassau Bay

When we finally moved into our new home on Cape Charles, in Nassau Bay, Texas, it was incredible. This was an exclusive area just across the street from the National Aeronautics and Space Administration, NASA, which was the epicenter for the space program. It was during the Apollo years when we were sending astronauts to the moon, and this was the neighborhood where many of them lived with their kids.

This was a great place for us in so many ways. There were woods filled with big, old oaks with moss, birds, and shade. Galveston Bay wound its way back to the subdivision, and there was a freshwater fishing lake in the back.

Evans became my best friend almost instantly, and we were inseparable. You know the kind of best friends your parents say, "You should just get married." We did everything together. I don't know what I would have done if it had not been for Evans. I needed a best friend. Not that we talked deep into the nights about our feelings, but we struggled with boyhood together and shared so many stories of life together.

I think that that friendship kept me alive in a lot of ways. Evans' parents had their problems as well. I remember a lot of struggles, but they held it together. Their door was always open to me, and I always felt welcomed.

When we moved into the new house, I switched to Webster Elementary in Webster, Texas. I rode a bus for the first time to school every day. It was a wild, weird new world. It was fifth grade. I was still living one foot in boyhood and innocence and the other beginning to wander away from what my heart knew as true and good and right. The boy I was when we finally got to Nassau Bay was not the boy on Indigo. I was living in a much bigger world, and I felt it spinning.

Gym class was never a favorite time for me. Except for those years in Little League, our family was anything but a big sports family. One day the gym teacher had us all outside and lined up on the athletics field. We were dressed out in shorts and tennis shoes. She told us we were going to run a 100-yard dash and what the school record was for that distance. She explained how to run and take the corners with speed. She finished her talk, stepped to the side, and blew her whistle.

I took off and pulled out in front early. I ran and stayed out front. It was easy; I had one guy pushing behind me, but I was in front. I let off a bit and cruised around the course and into the home stretch. I pushed into it a bit at the end, but I was never stressed or anxious to do my best. The coach clicked her stopwatch as I passed and told me I was just a few seconds from breaking the school record.

What? I was that close? You mean I could have pushed it the whole way and creamed the school record? I would have left a mark in the athletic books. It really bothered me that I did not give it a little bit more. Even today I think about not giving it my all that day. It made a big impression on me, but not in the way it could have. Not enough to pursue track in my future. I had no idea what that would take or look like. No one was encouraging me or asking me anything. In my eyes it was done; I failed and chose anxiety.

At some point that same year, one of my teachers challenged us to write a story and told us it was a school-wide contest with a five dollar first prize. Now I was never much of a reader. I had read one maybe two books by this time in my life, so reading and writing were foreign except when mandated by teachers and exclusive to the classroom Monday through Friday.

I had never written anything before, but I dug in. For some reason, I was all in on this. I wrote a four- or five-page story with pen and paper about a guy who was a scientist. His expertise was underwater studies, and he stayed alone in an underwater lab for long periods of time. One time, when he came up out of his underwater lab, the earth had been destroyed. All the people were gone, vanished. The closing line was "My God, what is happening." I won the contest.

This was a big deal. I don't know that I had ever won anything before. The story was to be read in front of the whole school during an assembly. I had the option to read it myself or have someone else do it. I chose a popular kid who was pretty smart and I thought might be a good reader. Wrong. I stood to the side of the stage thinking the whole time he read it, "Say that real loud, pause, slowly read that detail." In my mind, all I could think was he was terrible; that was not how it needed to be read. I wanted a do-over. But the school clapped, and I got my five bucks. I made an unspoken vow at that point that I would never let anyone read my work again. If I ever had a chance to have something read, I would do it myself and do it with passion and zeal—even if I didn't know what that meant.

Being in the NASA neighborhood, we grew up with kids whose dads were flying around the moon. One of those was my close friend, Tom Gordon, whose dad just happened to be the pilot on Apollo 12—the second group of astronauts to go to the moon.

Tom was a funny kid with a great sense of humor. I remember once when his parents were traveling after his dad's Apollo flight, we were in his house raiding the refrigerator and exploring all the trinkets kings and presidents around the world had given to his dad. These were amazing and beautiful things like a perfect rose dipped in gold. It was beautiful.

NASA was pretty fun on some days, but most days it was just NASA. It was just the place across the highway that controlled the rocket ships to the moon. We walked across the street and into the heart of the NASA complex lots of times. We saw the antigravity machine, the spinning capsule, and all the training rooms and computer centers. We never got stopped or asked what we were doing; we explored freely.

On the south end of Nassau Bay was a small entrance into the subdivision. On the east side of the entrance, just across from NASA, was a resort, and I think it was called Nassau Bay Resort Inn. This was the nicest hotel around, and anytime something amazing was going on in space, the place was hopping. On top of the hotel was an ABC television studio. It was live the whole time any space flights were happening, and we went there many times and watched the action. Again, they never gave us much grief and would allow us to see everything. That was cool.

Near the front of the neighborhood on the main street was the shopping center and a small pancake house. We would occasionally sit at the counter drinking soda or water. One such afternoon was after a long day fishing and throwing the casting net in the bay. For some reason, I had a small shrimp in my pocket. I was a boy who had been fishing all day. What would you expect? We opened up the catsup bottle in front of us and stuffed the shrimp inside. We left pretty soon after and never saw the reaction, but I am betting it was super funny to the staff there. I don't remember going back.

On the other side of the road was the shopping center. The long row of maybe a dozen shops included a grocery, a drug store, miscellaneous other shops, and a smorgasbord cafeteria. We had all types of activities that kept us busy in Nassau Bay's commerce area.

One of our favorite day trips was to start at one end of the strip center and work our way to the other, stealing at least one thing from every store. I don't recall why we started to live a life of crime and terror, but it became a pretty regular routine. Neither Evans nor I were into sports or after school activities, so I am guessing it was out of boredom. We never stole really big stuff, mostly things we could use in the woods.

Another well-rehearsed activity was trading in pop and milk bottles for cash. Back in those days, milk came in big glass bottles you could bring to the grocery store and collect a cash deposit. It was the same with coke bottles. There were times we would actually have a few, but for the most part, we lied about bringing them in. It was the honor system, and that worked perfectly for us. We would take the small amount of cash and buy food to eat as we sat in the shade against a tree in the woods.

They eventually got our number on the scams and would not give us money. That was okay; we were bored with them anyway. The adrenaline stopped flowing, and it was going to take bigger and more devious thinking to have any fun.

5

Late Nights
and Puppies

Other kids were in and out of our circle of influence. One boy whose name I do not remember lived near me and visited one Christmas day on his shiny new ten-speed bike. It was top of the line, and he was proud to show it off. I remember I was jealous of his bike the minute I saw it. I didn't get anything even close; Mom and Dad were trying, but things were tight. As soon as he finished saying, "Like my new bike," I started telling my story. I told him I got a new one too, almost just like his, but unfortunately, it was already in the shop getting fixed. Yes, on Christmas day a bike repair shop was open somewhere. For weeks after that he would ask to see it, and I always had a new excuse. I am sure after a while he just did it to hear me lie to him and to relate my ignorance to his friends and family. I don't know why I said that. I felt that shame of lying for years.

We would sneak out and run around at night. Sometimes we would meet other kids, maybe even a girl, but mostly just us goofing around. I remember one night Evans and I had slipped out of his bedroom window to run the streets. We were gone for a couple of hours just hiding from cars and walking. When we were heading back, we heard sirens, and as we got closer, we saw all the action was next door to his house. The neighbor's house had caught on fire, and everyone was standing out front, including his parents. We walked up acting like we had just come from inside, busted. They had already looked everywhere for us. Boys will be boys; we just went inside and fell asleep.

Galveston Bay flowed into an inlet called Nassau Bay not far from the house. I loved that. Mom and Dad knew I was drawn to fishing and over time, they helped me acquire all types of fishing gear. I would load a wagon and pull my fishing gear, nets, and snack to the water's edge and spend the day fishing. It was a glorious time for me. Most of the fish I caught were just bottom feeders, but I didn't care. I remember one really good day I caught a nice redfish. It was big at the time and, thinking about it now, I never even considered size or any other limits or rules. It was fishing at its finest. I had a casting net I learned to throw there. I was captivated by all the small live things it brought in— shrimp, fish, jellyfish, and crabs.

Our family decided we would get a puppy for the new house. It was really more that I finagled my parents into a puppy, and once we had one, he never left my side. We had had dogs in the past, but this was different. This one was mine, and Dad assured me I was fully responsible. No problem, I could do this. I was overwhelmed with joy; I was a boy with his dog. One day I had loaded all my fishing gear into the wagon and made my way to the bayside. It was a beautiful day, and I could not imagine much of anything I wanted except to maybe catch a big fish. As I laid in the long, cool grass on the banks of my favorite fishing spot near the docks, my puppy ran up the incline and into the street. I heard a screech and a thump. I jumped up to see my dog lying underneath a car stopped on the road. I ran and picked him up. Crying and in shock, I ran all the way home with him in my arms. Mom loaded us up and took us to the vet. I don't think he was alive when we got there; he didn't come home with us.

A few weeks later, my dad came into my room and handed me an envelope. What, mail, I got mail? It was a bill from the veterinarian hospital, and he told me it was my responsibility to pay it. I didn't know what to say or do. I was just a kid.

I finally figured out I would take all the change I had saved and put it in the envelope and mail it to them. I struggled to get it all to fit and keep from falling out the edges. It wasn't much, maybe ten dollars, but it was a start. I licked and taped and put a stamp on it. A few weeks later I got a second bill reflecting the payment. The postage due almost exceeded the amount of change I had packed in the little white envelope they received. The lessons my heart learned from the experience were hard. Oh, and I learned you don't mail change. Nobody told me anything about that either.

Our home was surrounded by towering oaks and palms. One day while goofing around in the backyard, there on the ground were two baby owls. Strange. Being the animal expert I was, I immediately picked them up and found a box for them. Mom was not real pleased, but we took up caring for them. Trial and error were our teachers.

We had seen the mom and heard the parents, but we didn't know to do anything but try and raise these babies. Obviously, the parents were careless and needed our help. One of the babies died pretty quickly. But the other grew strong. It wasn't long until we took him out back, and he flew off into the oak tree where his parents had sat so many nights. Just a day or two later, we received the thanks for caring for him. Dead mice, pieces of dead animals, regurgitated, raw, whole dead things on our back picnic table where we played with him so often. Wow, how cool was that. He was thanking us.

There was a large area of woods that ran along a part of the bay. We called it Gaston's Woods, and it was a haven for exploration and a great hideout to learn all the things boys learn in the woods. Shooting at each other with BB guns (picket fights) was typical. Today kids use air soft guns that shoot small plastic BB's. We used real BB guns. We built campsites and tree forts. We learned that throwing aerosol cans in a fire caused a pretty catastrophic explosion. We explored debris that washed up on the shores from Galveston Bay and beyond.

There were nights we would camp out there in the woods. The nights were long, and the gear modest to non-existing. It was more about finding drugs or alcohol and the fire. There was also what we called the sunrise service. I am sure it was modeled in some weird way after the Catholic services we knew, but they concluded with pure boyhood antics. The interesting thing to me is that it was even part of our thought process. There was no God conversations or prayers to speak of, maybe a still quiet moment of reflection as the sun rose, but then it returned to normal programming of exploding aerosol cans, fire, and beans cooked on an open flame.

One day, I found myself following one of my brother's best friends, Steve, through the woods. It was a normal day, and trailing one of my brother's friends was not out of the norm for me. My intention was to try and join in on some drugs he might have. We followed a trail to the left then to the right; we went straight then under branches and around a tree or two. Then he stopped. He turned and looked at me straight in the eyes and said, "You just followed me around in a circle." He laughed, and I placed a marker in my mind. I would never follow anyone blindly again—never.

There was also an incredible freshwater lake in the back of the neighborhood. It wasn't real big, maybe ten acres. The edges of the lake were lined with jagged granite, and on the south end, a covered pier was accessible through a small public park. One day I was fishing away, and I caught an alligator gar. He was a mean, long, skinny, and ugly brute, and it took everything to fight him onto the rocks. An older fellow fishing near me saw the commotion and came over to cheer me on.

Just as I was pulling the mean ole gar up on the rocks, my line slid across a sharp edge and pop, it broke. The older guy immediately jumped onto the rocks and fought to grab the fish and throw it up on shore. He was determined not to let it get away, and he didn't. He killed that fish and explained they were bad for the lake and needed to be taken out. It was one of my first outdoor lessons on conservation, and it came lakeside by a stranger. That was a cool day for fishing.

My dad bought a boat while we were living in the new house. We had a lot of fun learning to water ski and traverse the salty waterways. There was so much to explore, and the boat opened up a whole new view of outdoor adventure.

The tri-hull Glastron was great for everything we did. Eventually, Dad let John take it out with his friends, and occasionally Evans and I would be invited. We skied and roamed the channels and backwaters. During the summer, there were all kinds of activities happening along the shoreline, and we were there. John was a really good water skier, and so were his friends. They could use one ski, two skis, or no skis jumping the ramp.

Old man Doc brought in a ski hut and floating dock. He taught skiing classes, and we were there a lot. We weren't always taking classes but hanging out. One day my little sister, Cathy, was there with me. We were on the ski dock when somehow we both ended up in the water. She struggled and grabbed me—climbing on me and fighting to get out of the water while pushing me under. It was the classic drowning person drowning the person with them. I could see the light green water above but couldn't get there. I thought for that moment, clearly in my mind, I was going to drown right then and there. As I completed that thought and considered life in Purgatory with no knowledge if I would be able to make it any higher, someone lifted us out of the water.

I loved that small town and all it had to offer. Even though life was hard, there were things that clearly defined who I would be, and they were not all bad. But this was also when I began to use drugs. As time progressed, it did not matter what kind of drugs or when, I just used. Thinking back on that young boy, rudderless, where was Dad? Where was Mom?

6

Stepping In

Then the transition came. Stepping up into the plebe role in middle school. Going from top dog in elementary to just a punk kid in middle school. It all seems so innocent. It should be joyful and celebrated. It should have been Mom and Dad talking about the transition, what it will be like, asking how it was going. This should be good, big brother in eighth grade and me in sixth.

Middle school was where the world I knew as a boy really began to unravel. This is a really tough time for a boy, and I don't remember anyone monitoring or talking to me about how I was doing or what it would look like in the next phase of boyhood. I can see now how that would have helped a lot. My eyes were already open to new things—things that intrigued me like drugs, cigarettes, and girls. It seems like such a young age now, but then it seemed natural. What little fear there may have been about stepping into those things was stuffed way down inside. The need to be a part of something, to have meaning, and to be accepted was far too important.

Looking back on it now, I think many adults around me were alcoholics or using drugs. The dads drank, and the moms took all types of pills if they were not drinking. Our brothers were blazing the trails ahead of us in all those directions, so we followed. It is what a little brother does so often.

Sniffing all types of chemicals was one of our first experiments. The one we used most was butane lighter fluid. The cans you use to refill a butane lighter were easily accessible and affordable if we did not steal one from our parents or a local store.

This was an incredibly dangerous way to get high. Not only was there a chance we would just drop dead, but also lots of brain cells died every time we did it. Another crazy fact about using that drug was the terrible aftereffect that followed just minutes later of a hangover, headache, and dizzy, nasty feeling. Even with that, we always did it again, and again, and again. It was gross.

Cigarettes were right in that same time. It was a warm summer day the first time I smoked—off in the woods somewhere I am guessing. When we were walking back home, I got really sick, super dizzy, and nauseated. It was horrible, and I hated it. The only way to get everything to stop spinning was to lie down on the concrete sidewalk. I laid there for a long time. My friends had little patience and left me. I didn't care. I would never do that again—until the next day. I smoked for over twenty years.

Life at home continued to get bad although the problems between my parents were almost always hidden from us kids. I heard stories long after we had become adults. Mom told about Dad and his physical attacks on her, which resulted in deeper more serious mental and physical wounding, his drinking, chasing other women, and forcing her to sleep with him when he was drunk.

Webster Intermediate was where the bus dropped us off every day for the sixth through eighth grades. I got serious about drugs and girls and all the social influences that came with being in the big school. John was two years ahead of me, so he had a reputation as well as his friends and my friends' brothers. I remember feeling proud to be the little brother of an important eighth grader and probably a bit arrogant or condescending knowing I had backup from that level.

Almost every day included smoking pot and cigarettes—before school at the bus stop, sneaking off campus, or finding nooks and crannies around the school. I had a good friend, John Grant, who was struggling to find his way in life as desperately as I was. In school, we took turns bouncing off each other's stupidity. We had one class together I regret. It was art class.

I am pretty good at drawing. I drew mostly cartoon figures, but I spent hours drawing in school so an art class would seem like a place I would actually thrive. The problem was John and I together was not a good mix. I remember the teacher was young and pretty. We both had a bit of a crush on her. We showed our care for her one day when we stole spray adhesive and took turns inhaling it to get completely disoriented and high. Then we caused such a disruption in her class; we were so disrespectful that she ran out of the class crying. We were jerks.

The sixth grade became the testing grounds for many of my habits and behaviors that would become life staples for years. It was a formative time, and I had free rein. There were occasional consequences for my misbehavior but rarely.

I recognize that my heart, even in middle school, would temporarily open to things that would later be markers for who God wanted me to be. T.A.R.S., Teens Aid the Retarded, was a group that a couple of friends and I became a part of in middle school. Sadly, the program no longer exists, and of course, the name would never make it in society today. I don't know how or who thought I would fit there—as a volunteer anyway. The activities were simple. We would go to a building off campus where kids with learning disabilities were, and we would hang out with them, play games, and goof around. It got us out of class, and we could smoke weed on the way over. Although my memory of who I was with and any specific kids I helped is non-existent, I remember the feeling of helping and that I liked it. I also remember I didn't like that I got high before I went and wished I hadn't. But I did it every time.

My one and only fight ever at school was at about the same time. Another guy was picking on my friend, Tom Gordon, and I took up for him. I don't know why. Tom was my size, and I certainly was no badass. But I guess my mouth got out ahead of my brain, and I told this kid to meet me after school.

We skipped the bus home and met at the apartments next door to the school. There was a big grass courtyard area, and we squared off in the middle with other kids all around. Crash, we got into it. The next thing I remember was I was on top of him with his arms pinned down, and I had to make a decision whether I would start punching his face or not. I had him, he was down, and my arms, hands, and fists were free to smash away. At that moment, I was struggling with brutality. Then God stepped in as an old man from the complex. He came out and yelled at us, "Hey, what are you kids doing. Get out of here." That was my out. We all jumped up and ran away. That was that—my first fight was done; I won by default. Today, I know it was grace. I just could not bring myself to punch the face of that kid. I just couldn't.

One day in seventh grade, while sitting in class I had two girls accuse me of saying something inappropriate to them. Again, I can't recall the accusation, but it was bad enough for the teacher to send me to the principal. That was never good, and with my record, I was always teetering on suspension. I much preferred to sit in the back of the room, unnoticed, high or asleep. Better yet would be to slip off campus somewhere and not have to deal with any of it. But this was different. This time, I didn't do it. Whatever it was, I truly was innocent. The problem was my reputation and previous convictions did not give the school officials anything to stand on except that I was a little hippie stoner who lied, skipped classes, and didn't care about much of anything. So when I expressed my innocence, it did not get far.

They called my dad. He was summoned to the school, and he was mad. I was given a minute to talk with him before we went before the vice-principal, the disciplinarian, whom I feared. I explained to my dad that I didn't say it. I was innocent. I really was. That was when one of the most important things in my life occurred, he believed me and stood up for me. He was all in and insisted the girls were lying, and he would not tolerate my being punished for something that could not be proven. He stood with me and for me. I will never forget that feeling.

I know my dad loved me. We did all kinds of things together as a family. But this was different—it was him, for me, all in. I only remember one other time, at the ballfield, where he was engaged, in for me, just me. And he seemed sober this time. It made a huge impression that Dad was there for me, that he stood in the gap, and I mattered.

7

Bullies and Weed

School was a dangerous place in a lot of ways. A couple of guys were clearly the school bullies and did not like Evans or me. One guy was His-panic; they called him Jon-Jon. The other was Scott. Jon-Jon was a medium-build dude but had a tough exterior and didn't seem to care about much. Scott, his sidekick, was a big, fat, red-headed ole country boy. They were quite the pair and caused us a lot of grief. At one point, the bully-ing got to be too much, and we asked our brothers to step in and help us out.

Ah, the beauty of a big brother at its finest. John tried the diplomatic approach—talking, trying to compromise and getting the guys to lay off. Wyatt, Evans' older brother, tried a different approach. He met them on the tennis court and whipped their butts. I remember watching and feeling uncomfortable. Wyatt got his shirt stretched a bit, but he was a bad dude—fast, smart, and mean when it came to these kinds of things. And that was it. We never had a prob-lem again. We slowly became friends in some weird way with Jon-Jon and Scott. Our big brothers took on another level of admiration in our eyes.

That summer Dad sent the family off to Galesburg, Illi-nois, to visit my mom's mom. We rode the train up there every few years, and that was fun. This year, however, I had some information I just knew was accurate. I heard there were legal marijuana farms in the area. I was told through well-trusted sources that the government grew a lot of it, and if you looked hard enough, you would find them and maybe even be able to steal some from the edges. I looked everywhere I could around that little small town. The whole county was cornfields, so it only made sense there would be weed planted every other row. Nothing.

I was walking down the railroad tracks one afternoon after exploring the south end of town for government weed farms when I saw it right there on the side of the track. Weed must grow wild all along the railroad tracks in Illinois, I thought. The seeds must fly off the train car loads of pot going to the government weed processing centers and fall all along the tracks. It was tall, lush, and I harvested it—lots of it.

I was nervous as a long tail cat in a dance studio the whole train ride back. My suitcase was stuffed and smelled like an oregano factory. I was sure I would be busted. We finally made it home, and how my mom never found out or questioned the bulging, smelly suitcase, I will never know. I immediately snuck all the greenery to the side of our garage and laid it out to sun dry. This was going to be good.

Two days later, a midnight knock on our door woke the house. Dad came into my room and ordered me to the den. I was confused. My brothers and sisters scrambled to see what was going on. I lagged behind but pushed my way to the front and entered the brightly lit room. There, standing next to the pool table were two Sheriff officers and a bunch of wilted green plants lying across the top. What the heck. Someone narked on me.

Apparently, I had shown or told someone about my crazy find, and they told their parents. I guess there was a lucky side to this whole thing because it wasn't marijuana; it was milkweed. I had done all that work and worried that whole time. I was mad and glad in the same instant. My parents grounded me after that, but those things never meant anything. Those cops were pretty smug but firm. I guess I was not looking very remorseful. A seventh grader trying to make a few bucks, what was the problem, old people? Relax.

On another night when my parents were out, I was at home alone. I don't know how it was I was alone. For almost all my memories as a kid back then, I have no memories of my little brothers and sisters being around. I am guessing it is that I was a young teen and self-consumed, but that is just a guess.

I knew that week that John had scored some good acid (LSD). I went looking for it with the intent of stealing a bit of it. Finding your brother's hiding places did not take that much effort. We both thought and talked about spots to hide things, and since we shared a room, it wasn't long til I found it. It was a neatly folded piece of foil and inside were pieces of a broken pill. It was like an orange baby aspirin. I had thought he said he bought Orange Sunshine LSD, an especially strong type available back then, and it turns out he did.

I had never taken LSD before, but I wasn't afraid to try. Even with all the things I had heard about this particularly strong type, it did not bother me at all. There were several small broken pieces off the main pill, so I took one out, ate it, and returned the hidden package to its lair.

Somehow I found my way into my parents' room and fell asleep on their bed before anything happened. All I remember is my parents waking me up and asking me what drugs my brother had taken and what I knew about it. I was confused and incoherent; the drugs had kicked in while I was asleep. I told them I had no idea what he did, and they sent me to my room where I spent the night in a fog of confusion and fear.

John, on the other hand, had been having quite the night until the cops arrested him and Steve Bowcock. They had taken quite a bit of the powerful orange tablet and were over the top. They were manic and crazed. The cops had them, and they had lost control of just about everything including, rumor has it, their bodily functions. John got grounded for that one.

Even with all that scariness and insanity, we continued to take acid. I took some at school one day, and I remember the walls breathing and totally being out of my mind. How it was that my teachers did not pick up on a seventh grader out of his mind, I don't know. Just the confusion and inability to speak should have been a sign.

Evans and I shared a lot of acid. We traveled the community during these acid trips. We would explore the woods, lie under the trees, and dig through Goodwill boxes for stuff. Back then you didn't take your old household goods or clothes to a Goodwill store; there were boxes set up in church parking lots. You would just drop the clothes in a door on the top in the front. One night we were experiencing a high dose of LSD when we came across a Goodwill box. We always accessed the back and explored the discarded items, and this time we scored. We found an extra large silk boxer's robe. It was a big gold and yellow robe with the fighter's name on the back. It was huge.

We took turns getting on each other's shoulders, wearing the robe to look like a huge man. This guy must have been huge, but for a couple of hours, we were about as goofy as we ever got.

We also ate psilocybin mushrooms we picked ourselves that grew in the cow pastures everywhere around us. Being highly skilled at plant identification made this a no-brainer. I would go out and eat wild mushrooms with the possibility I might eat a highly poisonous one and die. Lucky for me that never happened, but looking back on it I don't know why it didn't.

I don't want this to be funny, but some of it is. Really, it was stupid. As I write all this, I feel a strange emotion of anger and fear mixed together. Why was I out doing all these things unnoticed? How did I pay for things? It was so dangerous. Gabriel was working overtime for my mom watching over me.

Gradually any pill or drug was of interest and not hard to come by. In south Houston, drugs were sold in the open on Sunday afternoons in Milby Park. We would hitchhike down there and walk the open trails. Alongside the trails were different folks each with different drugs. If you had money, you could score your weekly drug fill right then and there. From what I read now, there were lots of concerts in the park, but we never went there for the music. Eventually, there was a huge bust, and everything stopped.

On one of our many trips to the park, Evans and I rode with our brothers in Steve's Rambler. After filling our pockets with the desired drugs of choice for the day, we started the return trip back. Headed down the road, we smelled something burning. Smoke started billowing from the back seat. We rolled the windows down, and Steve pushed the little Rambler to its limits down the highway trying to get to a gas station or someplace with a water hose. We finally whipped into a station and doused the back seat with water. Apparently, the ash from a cigarette had dropped off between the seats and caused quite the smoldering mess. It was a few minutes after we had put the burning mess out when we realized how stupid it all was—racing down the road, smoke billowing out of the car, and everyone with pockets full of drugs.

8

Girls

For some reason along the way, Dad's income or debt took its toll, and we had to sell the home my parents had built. It was never a family conversation or topic I can remember. We just rented a house on the other side of Nassau Bay and moved. The big white house.

This is where the end of the family began. It is where I realized there was a real problem. I had free rein from the rented white house. I came and went, snuck out using the front door, and never asked permission.

I can't imagine the feeling of failure and shame my parents must have carried—especially for Mom having to operate in the neighborhood circles after the move. My parents really never had neighbors as friends; we didn't do things with anyone in the neighborhood as families. We occasionally went to the Catholic church there, and surely they saw neighbors there or at the grocery store. Shame is a devastating mistress.

One thing I remember clearly, so much that it placed a marker in my senses was a pungent odor inside the house of stale cigarettes and booze. It seeped from the pores of my father, and in the mornings, it was prevalent throughout our home. To this day, I can recall the odor and how it followed him. It seems hard to write about, but it defines an element of that white house in my memory.

On Indigo, I knew a few girls and tried my best to lure them into a compromising situation. In Nassau Bay, I remember once getting a girl into the boat which was stored in the garage at the time. I pushed myself on her and tried my best to figure out how to move along the bases. It was awkward, and there was nothing romantic or thoughtful about it. It was all about me. There were a few girls back then who must have been starving for affection, because at the time I can never remember caring about any of them past my selfish desire to try and do something I didn't know how to do. It breaks my heart today, but it was just the beginning.

One night I ended up at the movies in Clear Lake. It was just a quick hitchhike away and the only movie house around. I went there to look for girls and watch a movie. On this particular night, the movie *Taxi Driver* was playing. I was totally drawn in to the movie and fell head over heels in love with Jody Foster. In some deep emotional way, I wanted to rescue her. I wanted to save her and care for her. I had no idea what that meant, but it was there inside of me. When we left the movies, I walked around the streets alone yelling her name. It was a strong, emotional night; I longed for something, and I thought it was her.

There were other girls along the way. If a girl showed me any attention at all, I fell in love. I have found love letters and notes I wrote to them back then. They seem to be typical boyhood crush stuff.

Brown-Eyed Girl

X

My first attempt at running away came because I was vulnerable to the emotions of my heart. A girl owned me. Today her name escapes me, but the experience does not. The dark-haired, brown-eyed girl had captured my heart at school. We never dated, we never exchanged spit, or did anything physical. But somewhere along the way, she gave me a note or passed along through a friend that she liked me, and that was all it took. The announcement that her family was moving was sudden, and then she was gone. Her family moved to Lake Jackson, Texas, which is about an hour's drive south of Nassau Bay. It wasn't real far, but it seemed like a million miles. For some reason, I decided she was worth chasing at all costs, so I planned it.

After a few weeks, I had gathered a pocket full of change and some bills and found my way to a bus station. The Greyhound system worked well, and people used it. The stations and busses may not have been pristine, but I never noticed anything that made me think twice. My turn came at the ticket window, and I stepped up for a ticket. "Lake Jackson, please," not a problem. I didn't think of a round trip ticket, and when he asked me, I had to think a minute. I pulled out all my money and that made the decision for me—I could only go one-way.

There were never any requests for identification or anything. I got a ticket and got on the bus. The distance was short, but it took a while to get there. The bus stopped in every little town along the way to shuffle folks on and off.

53

Finally, I arrived. It was Saturday afternoon, and the day was warm and sunny. When I got off the bus, I stood there a minute trying to figure out where I was and what to do next. I went inside and asked a counter representative if they knew the apartments where I was headed. They did; it was not far. Lake Jackson was a small town, and there was only one apartment complex.

My heart raced as I walked, anticipating the reunion and how excited she would be that I left everything to come and be with her. I was also confused inside. Where was I, and what was I doing? Everything around me was blurry without texture or meaning. I had one thought and emotion moving me forward.

I arrived at the apartments and wandered around until I found her unit. A set of stairs led up to her front door, and her little sister was sitting on the steps. I stood in front of her on the ground floor level. Elton John's "Madman Across the Water" was blaring from her apartment. I asked her little sister where she was. She told me she was inside with her new boyfriend and she had been kicked out. She told me that whenever she had a boyfriend over she got kicked out and her sister would play that record real loud until she could come back in.

I sat there, the music playing, dumbfounded, numb. I left before the music ended. I hitchhiked back home.

Then there was Robin. Robin did not fit the mold. I was head-over-heels for Robin, and she liked me too. I didn't know anything about dating or courting a girl. But I tried to spend time with her. The difference with Robin was she was a good girl. She lived at home with her parents, went to church, wouldn't fool around, and made it real clear. I cared a lot for Robin, but we didn't last long. I don't know if it was her parents or her moral values, but it eventually ended in heartbreak for me. Looking back now, I think she must have been a Christian. Her parents were raising her to be strong, and it had taken. It was a foreign concept to me. I love that now; I am so happy I did not interrupt that.

Sharon was my sister's friend. She was a twin and lived in Friendswood, another suburb down the highway a few miles. I was awestruck, a common emotion for me with a girl then. She became what I thought was my first real love. I did everything I could to find an excuse to be around her.

She was thin and had straight brown hair and a square nose. Her smile, her laugh, drew me in. She filled so many of my broken needs, and her mom was always open to caring for me too. Not having a dad in the house was a hardship on her family. The house needed healthy masculinity, but as much as I desperately wanted to offer that and rescue them, I had no clue. We both made bad choices and did things that hurt each other. I have to say she was my biggest heartbreak over and over again. But time and time again, she was there. I am happy to say to this day she is one of my oldest and dearest friends. I am proud of the fact we have remained friends. God's grace for me.

I began to understand and notice Dad's drinking more while we were living in the old white house. I would find random empty bottles of rum in strange places. Once I remember hearing what sounded like marbles spill out on the floor with a loud crash. I ran to the foot of the stairs to find Dad lying there. He had fallen down the stairs onto the tile floor, drunk. We joked about him "losing his marbles." To this day I don't know what made that sound, but it was clear and audible, and it bothers me when I think about it.

There was a little fort we built in the backyard. The lot had a V-shaped corner, and it didn't take much to put boards down for a makeshift floor and roof. A lot of drugs and experimenting with girls took place in that corner. There was also an alley between the houses there in that corner, and we used it to travel secretly about the neighborhood. Just on the other side of the back fence was the Nassau Bay Inn.

One night, for whatever reason, Dad rented hotel rooms for my brother and me at the inn. I had no idea why, but I was not asking questions. Evans and I hitchhiked over to Sharon's and tried our best to lure her and her sister to the hotel—no luck. It was late when we finally gave up and started our walk back. What the heck, we had a hotel room and nothing to do. No girls, no drugs, nothing. As we walked along the highway, I looked down and on the side of the road was a baggy of something. I picked it up and was thrilled it was weed. What the…? We were whooping and hollering. It wasn't going to be such a bad night after all. We made our way back to the hotel, and it must have stunk to high heaven shortly after.

I am not sure why Dad rented us those rooms, but I have heard stories that that night my dad got drunk and tried to strangle my mom. As they struggled, my little brother walked into their room. It saved her life.

For years, Mom had tried to salvage the marriage with Al-Anon meetings, priests, and little yellow pills. I knew about the pills and took full advantage of her supply. Sometimes in relationships like the one my parents had, you have to call uncle to rescue the kids or stay alive.

Taking drugs, skipping school, mistreating my teachers, and just being an idiot continued all the way through middle school up to the last day of eighth grade when I got in trouble walking to the bus. This was my last day to be at this hell hole, this place that did not understand me. This place where I perceived I was bullied by students, jocks, and teachers. This place where I became so cool, and everyone else became so lame. I just had to make it to the front of the school, get my graduation certificate, get on the bus, and get the heck out of there. I didn't make it. I got in trouble between the building and the bus. The evil vice-principal saw it and ushered me onto the bus without my certificate and gave a clear verbal message. "You screwed up, and you're not getting this certificate." Crap, I could not do even that? I cared, but then, screw it; I really didn't. It was over.

Early that summer, Mom announced she was divorcing Dad and moving to Illinois. The big white house would have to be vacated by a certain date, and I was to be ready to move. I was crushed. As dysfunctional and unhealthy as my life was, it was my life, and I made it clear I was not moving. Mom packed everything, and one day it was all gone. She left. I had refused to go, and she left me, she really left.

Dad was gone now too. He collected what was left and his bottle of rum and just moved away. I know Mom was trying to rescue the little ones. John and I would have to be casualties of the divorce. Not by her choice; I am sure we could have gone, but we were having none of it. Dad never invited me.

The house sat empty as I looked around. I didn't know where John had gone. I was going to have to figure something out. I spent the last night in the house. No electricity, no furniture, nothing but me, alone in the big white house.

9

Summer's Over

To top it all off, at the beginning of that summer, Evans' family moved to California. His dad got a job near Lake Arrowhead, so they moved. My world was crashing in on me, and I had to deal with a lot of tough stuff. I knew it was up to me to stay alive, to make it happen, whatever that was.

My big brother was old enough to get a job at the pizza restaurant and began to work and got an apartment. I wandered the streets sleeping at friends' houses, in Goodwill boxes, or wherever I could find a place. My drug use had grown to include injecting cocaine and anything that could be melted down. I was a lost boy in a lonely place. It is sad thinking about a boy that age without a man to help him find his way.

That summer came to an end when the first day of high school came around. I got on the bus with everyone and rode to the campus. My friends went in different directions, and I wandered the halls watching the crowds of kids. It was the big league. When the bell rang, the halls cleared. I watched my friends disappear into their classrooms. I wasn't registered. I had no one to call. I walked out the side door and down the street. School was over.

There was a girl I had fallen for who had also moved to California. She was a pretty blonde, tall with thin long hair. Leanne. Her sister was a friend of my brother, and they partied a lot. Leanne and I liked each other, and her parents let us spend time together. I had a brilliant thought at that moment. I would go to California.

I don't think I gave hitchhiking to California much of a thought. The trip would be a long one, and money was slim. I hoped the people who gave me a ride would be nice. One of my brother's friends, Terry, liked Leanne's sister, and he agreed to go with me. We didn't have to wait long to get our first ride. A guy in an RV picked us up, and the journey began.

It is traditionally polite to talk with the driver who picks you up. You can sum up who they are pretty fast and decide what story you will give them. You can change where you are going and what you need. Usually, you tell them your plan, ask who they are. A lot of times people really cared; they were encouraging and thoughtful. There were also the ones who didn't care. Did you have any gas money, got any food, or can you drive? It was all about the mission of getting where they were going. A great ride on a long trip would be the semi-trucks with sleepers. Some guys would let one of you sleep, and the other would talk with him.

There were always the creeps who had other things in mind. It was not unusual to get picked up by an older homosexual male. The gay guys almost always had other ideas in their head and that could, if you were smart, play to your advantage. They would be willing to buy you food, give you money, and take you farther than their exit. But there was always the question somewhere along the way, do you want to go to their place or get a hotel room. I never allowed myself to be taken advantage of or let my guard down where I was so loaded or tired and needy that I woke up to find myself in a compromised situation. Life had become a complicated game of survival.

Stepping out that day onto Interstate 10 was the first time I really recognized the interstate system of major travel routes crisscrossing the country. One complication was not being able to actually get down on the interstate in a lot of areas. The on-ramps had signs keeping pedestrians from walking along the main road. Sometimes we paid attention to them, other times not. Another complication was never knowing where you might get left off. It was never enough to keep us from traveling.

The trip from Houston to Los Angeles was a long trip. We caught a few different rides along the way. There was an RV, a semi-truck, and a few cars as we made our way west. Finally, we made it to the edge of the Mojave Desert. It was summer, dry, and hot. We stood at a gas station where the outside thermometer in the shade showed it was 110 degrees. It was hot.

We managed to convince a couple headed our direction to let us ride in the back of their pickup. We didn't have any sunscreen or tarp or cover of any kind. We sat on our clothes and backpacks to keep off the skillet-hot bed. The one saving grace, or it seemed that way at the time, was a bottle of Southern Comfort whiskey Terry had bought. We drank on that as we headed out Interstate 10 into the desert. I passed out.

I awoke hours later, fried and stiff. My skin was tender and as red as a ripe tomato. Before I knew it, we were in bumper-to-bumper traffic and rolling into Los Angeles. It took most of the day to find our way to the posh neighborhood the girls lived in. When we finally arrived, they snuck us into a room in the back of their house, fed us, and we got a shower. It was obvious they didn't want Mom and Dad to know we were around. That was OK with us. My tender burned skin and weary body and mind found a corner, and I went out, curled up in the fetal position.

We were awakened the next day with the girls ready to head to the beach. We loaded into a new car and headed out without food or concern for anything but some fun. It wasn't long before the aroma of California weed filled the car. We parked along the highway at a trailhead leading down a cliff to the rolling waves and sandy beach below. A sign at the beginning of the trail read, "Clothing Optional Beach." What the heck was this? It didn't take long for me to figure it out. Young and old folks alike laid around, walked around, mingled uninhibited by their nakedness. I was a bit freaked out. I never disrobed fully, but everyone else did.

After a day at the nude beach, we went back to the girls' house and ate. I was famished, and the food stopped the growling and helped bring me down from all the pot and beer of the day. Leanne and I never really experienced a spark. I had a huge fantasy before we arrived, but none of it played out. We barely kissed or held hands. It was clear I was a novelty, a piece of a now past life that she was moving on from.

The next morning, I decided I would go see Evans. He had moved to Arrowhead, California, and it was not that far. With little fanfare or emotion, I walked down the street and out to the highway. I stuck out my thumb and almost immediately caught a ride. "Where ya going, dude," was the question from the young guy who picked me up. "Arrowhead," I replied. "Crazy man, that is exactly where I am headed. Must be your lucky day." I participated in the obligatory talking all the way to Arrowhead. For hours and hours. I was still tired and tender from the sunburn on my body from the desert and naked beach. While I was nodding in and out and my head was bobbing from the sleepiness, we made our way up into the mountains.

When we arrived in Arrowhead, Evans and Wyatt came into town and picked me up. I felt safe there. His mom and dad loved me and knew I was not in a good place. With all the flaws and hardships their family faced with three rowdy teen boys, they got it. I was fed and got to stay without interrogation or pressure. I am tearful as I think about them today.

10

Arrowhead, Las Vegas, and Wyoming

Lake Arrowhead, California, was beautiful. Evans' house was an A-frame set in the mountains with tall pine trees and the resort and lake below. The temperatures were cool, a much-appreciated reprieve from the desert sun, beach, sand, and salt. The mountains have always been a retreat for me, and I loved it. The first few days I was healing from loneliness and the confusion that often entered my mind. Why am I doing this? Why do I have to be living this way? How come my friends are living in amazing houses in the mountains and going to school when my family sucks? It wasn't fair.

Evans and his brothers did not take long to find their way around Arrowhead. They showed me all the hangouts. They introduced me to the high quality and potent weed they had connected with. The pot was extra strong. It was different colors than what I was used to, and it was almost sticky. I learned a lot about the top quality pots available in California. A very high-end consumer product that not only smelled good and fresh, but it also had an amazing aroma as it burned, plus it got you really stoned.

The other California drug they had found quickly was LSD. All types of the drug were easily found, and I was open to trying them all. I wasn't afraid of any of it, and when they told me the "windowpane" acid was the strongest if placed in your eyelid to dissolve, I was game. We tripped a lot, and I have absolutely no memory of the adventures into oblivion.

After a few weeks, I could feel my time was short, and I needed to be heading out. I wasn't told to leave, but I was an inconvenience and a pretty bad influence on Evans and anyone who came around me. I called my mom thinking a visit to the family might be in order. Mom told me she was going with her uncle and my brother and sisters to Cody, Wyoming, for a vacation. She told me if I came and met them, I could go back to Illinois with them, and she would help me get established. She said maybe I could get a dirt bike like a lot of the boys around there or find something I would like. I was tired, and deep inside just wanted to be cared for and with my family.

I wasn't really sure where Cody, Wyoming, was but I found a map, got out on the highway, and hitchhiked. Rides came easily, and I got to Las Vegas quickly. It was the middle of the night when my latest ride dropped me off. The highway was never a good place to rest long. Finding a group of trees would be a good place to bunk out til daylight, but there was nothing. I was on the side of the highway in a town I did not know, and there was nothing. I was so tired I just could not stay awake. So I made the decision to curl up next to the guardrails and catch a few hours of sleep. Staying close to the highway I was going to head down made sense. I went out fast.

I don't know how much time passed, but the next thing I knew I was startled by a cop shaking me and telling me to wake up. He was parked next to the guardrail with his lights on. He started pounding me with questions. "Who was I? Why was I there? How old was I? Where was I going?" After a few questions, he figured out I was a minor and put me in his car. Crap, things were going to get messed up. This was not something I had thought about.

They called my mom, and she agreed to pay for me to fly one-way to Wyoming and would pick me up there. They cuffed me and drove me to the airport, walked me on the plane, and set me in my seat. Only after I was set in my seat did the monster cop uncuff me and point at my face, "Don't move." He didn't have to worry about that; I was done. As soon as he was gone, I pulled out my wallet and found the LSD, scratched it off the card, and swallowed it whole. Eventually, a little boy sat next to me, and the plane took off—and so did I.

I began tripping quickly, and it was very intense. The little boy got sick, and I marveled at his use of the barf bag. The plane was breathing in and out; every noise was amplified. When we finally landed in the small airport at Cody, Wyoming, my mom and sister were there to greet me. I don't know how I acted or what I looked like, but it had to be absolutely terrible. We made our way to a cabin in the woods, and I got my sister to go walk it off with me. What a terrible time to take LSD. How could I think it would be a good idea?

The rest of the time in Wyoming was uneventful. I began to eat again, and my body recovered from the long days and nights without any regular food or rest. Eventually, we left and made our way back to Galesburg, Illinois. My mom had moved into her childhood home with her mother. To us, she was "MiMi." PaPa had passed away years before, and this was a safe place for Mom to go to recover her life.

The house was small, and we kids bunked in the basement. It was me, my two sisters—Cathy, who is one year younger and Gen who is ten years younger—and Mike, my younger brother who is six years my junior. The house, comforts only a mom can offer, and cool days in Illinois were more of what I needed. The problem is I continued to listen to the demons inside and gravitated to the dark side of almost everything.

Before the family split, Cathy and I went into the hospital together. She got her tonsils out, and I had a deviated septum fixed (I have the bone chips to this day). The doctor who did my nose work was cutting edge, and one thing he pioneered was two plastic stents sutured into place to keep the scar tissue at a minimum. He would later remove them as part of his procedure.

While we were in Illinois, I continued to have trouble breathing, so Mom took me to the local general practitioner. He was checking me out, checking my ears, throat, and heart. Then he took a look in my nose to see how the work the specialist in Houston had come out. That is when he noticed the two stents, still in my nose. I didn't remember them being in there; Mom did not either. Ole Doc decided he needed to remove them, and he began to pull. I cussed up a storm, screaming in agony and anger. He went to a small cabinet and pulled out a small glass bottle, dipped a swab in it, and coated what he could in my nose. I asked him what it was, and I swear he said cocaine.

He finally pulled hard enough to get them out. That's when he discovered they were stitched into place. That was miserable. But I insisted we return soon after for a follow-up. I told Mom I wanted to go in and see ole Doc on my own. They put me in a room to wait and closed the door. I immediately jumped up and looked around til I found the vial of liquid cocaine. I also found a syringe, and I pocketed both and sat back down. The Doc came in, gave me the OK, and released me. I didn't feel nervous; I felt defiant. Life owed me anything and everything.

Back at MiMi's house after everyone had settled into the evening routine, I went into the single bathroom to shower. I took out the huge syringe; the needle was big, fat, and scary. It didn't matter. I opened the small bottle and drew up some liquid. How much? A lot or a little? I went in the middle. Tied off my left arm and inserted the needle.

The pain was almost immediate. Crushing, heart-throbbing pain. The liquid flowed through my body causing pain throughout. My mind raced; I am going to die. What did I do? What was that? I had done cocaine before, and this was not cocaine. I slowly came out of it and showered. I was sweating and hurting the rest of the night. Later, I found out that what I thought the doctor called cocaine was actually procaine, a topical numbing agent. It numbed things on the outside and had I done just a little bit more, I could have dropped dead right there on the bathroom floor. The fear of drugs and a life-ending lifestyle was short lived.

11

Same Thing, Only Different

Mom enrolled me in the local high school. I remember the first days there as a longhaired kid from Texas. The girls seemed to like me, but the guys hated me. I immediately found out who the drug users were and fell in with them. Drugs were plentiful, and I used them. There was a day when I was left at home, and I was looking for money. I found an old shoebox in my grandmother's closet full of old silver dollars. I took a pocket full and went to town. The guy's eyes at the little store opened wide as I went to pay for some miscellaneous crap with the coins. Of course, he took them; they were worth a lot of money, and I was cashing them in as dollars. To this day, I regret that. I used a lot of them for all types of things.

It didn't take long before I got in trouble at school and skipped classes. I spent all my time trying to bed girls and take drugs. I asked Mom one day about the motorcycle she said we would talk about, a dirt bike, but she did not remember the conversation. I am not sure if it was mostly me hearing things I wanted to hear, or if she never said it, but I took it as a betrayal, and it gave me something to anchor my rebellious attitude to.

That week I decided to go back to Texas. I took a handful of silver dollars and went to the train station and purchased a ticket. It was just a few minutes when the police showed up. They took me home. It must have looked pretty bad, a kid with a handful of antique silver dollars buying a ticket out of town in the middle of a weekday.

Officer Perez came to talk to me; he was in charge of juvenile law enforcement and delinquency. I decided to hate and dismissed him immediately. He warned me if I got in trouble again or missed another minute of school I would go to juvenile lockup. I skipped school Monday, and I was at the juvenile lockup facility on Friday. They locked me up in solitary confinement until Sunday. I remember looking out the window and thinking about how bad it would be to be locked up for an extended period of time. I wanted out.

The next weekend came, and I was running with the same crowd. We were drinking and drugging when someone had the idea to go break into the liquor store. It was after midnight, and the snow had stopped. Drifts were thick against the buildings as we made our way to the store. When we got there, we were all looking at each other. "So we're here, but now what?" Then crash, the front window broke from a brick striking dead center. A couple of the guys rushed in, my heart raced, and the alarm was screaming as I stood there. Then we heard a siren in the distance. We all took off in separate directions.

I didn't know what to do. I ran behind the store, cut to the left and along a fence line. I came to a chain link fence and climbed over it. There were scattered cars, apparently not working, parked all around. I slid under one in the wet snow and ice. I waited.

It wasn't long until I heard the police walking around. Their flashlights were shining in front of me, to the side, to the back. They were so close. I was shaking, wet, cold, scared, mad, and confused. Eventually, they left, but I stayed under the car for hours. Of course, they had followed my tracks in the snow, what an idiot. Why was I even there?

It was five in the morning when I tapped on the basement window and got my sister Cathy to let me in the house. I remember getting out of those cold, wet clothes into dry ones and crawling up into my top bunk bed. I curled into the fetal position and thanked God for getting me home. I was safe. That feeling was one I longed for.

The next week there was talk about the cops figuring out who broke into the liquor store. I was sitting in a classroom when I was called to the office. Jimmy, another accomplice, was in a chair just a few feet away. He told me they knew we broke into the store, and we were busted. I told him we should run. Just get up and bolt out of there. So we did. We ran across town to the house of a girl we knew liked us both. We partied at her house a lot. I don't know where her parents were, but it didn't seem to matter.

For the next two days, we consumed the most drugs I had ever taken. I blacked out for those two days. Somewhere along the way, I came out of it and knew I needed to get my stuff from the house and head back to Texas.

I will never forget that few minutes where I walked into the house after being gone for days without telling anyone. My mom must have been devastated. I ran into the basement, bagged up some clothes, and grabbed my shotgun. My dad had bought me a twenty-gauge pump before they split, and Mom had taken it with her. I came blowing up the basement stairs to my mom standing there crying. I must have looked crazed. She asked me to please not go, but I told her I had to. I said bye and left.

I went to the drug house and traded my shotgun for a bunch of PCP. Jimmy was there, and I told him I was headed out to Texas and he was welcome to come. He was in. Jimmy didn't have anything at home keeping him there. His dad was gone and his mom, well, she was a free spirit. We headed out the back alley and worked our way to the east side of town where I knew the trains passed regularly. I don't know where I came up with the idea of hopping a train; I had never done it before, and I had no idea where they were going. It didn't matter; I was going to Texas. It wasn't long before the next train slowed at the turn, and we hopped into an open car.

We really had no idea where a train would go, but this one headed south. There was no way to gauge what we were doing. We watched out of the door, hiding in the corners when we needed to. It was days later we realized we had made it most of the way to Texas. We hopped off in a small town and walked to the little general store. We had not eaten or had anything to drink in days. We ate honey buns and drank orange soda. We asked the lady behind the counter where we were, and she told us Oklahoma. I knew Oklahoma; we just needed to head south. We walked to the biggest road we could see and began walking, hitchhiking, and eventually caught enough rides to get us to Houston.

I called around and found a friend who would let us stay overnight at his mom's house. We made our way there, and it didn't take long for us to fall asleep. In the morning, Jimmy told me he was going to get cigarettes; I rolled over and kept sleeping. When I finally got up, I was alone. I wandered through the house—no one. I sat most of the day on the couch watching TV. No one came. In the late afternoon, I headed out. I did not want to be there when my friend's mom came home. I had no idea where Jimmy was, and my friend was still at school.

I hitchhiked back to the Nassau Bay area and wandered the streets and went to the woods, unsure of what I would do. After it got dark, I hitchhiked to Clear Lake City, just a few miles. I went to some places where I had known people—nobody. As it got later, I hid because I was a kid carrying a lot of drugs, and I could not be seen out that late or I would get stopped and probably thrown into jail. I finally called one of my brother's friends who I knew would welcome me because I had lots of good drugs. I remember walking across a field to his apartment in the tall, wet grass while it was dark. Every time a car came by, I crouched down to hide. It was a lonely walk, and I remember it very clearly. I don't know why but certain things happened in my life, moments that are so clear, I can feel the emotion of them today. I try not to go there; satan wants me to, but God is done with it.

I bounced around from apartment to apartment. I used the drugs to pay my way. I had divided it up into ten-dollar packets, and I had a lot of them. Then one day, I was staying with one of my brother's friends, and I remember being in the bathroom, shooting up, or trying to. He knocked on the door and asked what I was doing. He knew, but he asked. Then he opened the door and said, "Tom, you are losing it. You are shooting all your dope and screwing up big time. You need to go."

It was true. I had fallen into a place of real darkness and despair. I never left the apartment and I stayed stoned all the time. That moment crushed me, but it also launched me. I left and wandered from place to place. I remember breaking into a vet clinic and stealing lots of drugs. I injected all kinds of things I didn't even know. It didn't matter.

The drugs were always present, but my usage level went up and down. I tried to make sense out of things, and John offered to let me stay with him a while if I worked. He was always a good example of how to put it together. He got a job early and worked hard. Of course, he made his mistakes, used his fair share of drugs, and got in trouble. But through it all, and to this day, he has been a role model for me.

12

Coming to the End

John had just bought a new house, and the block he lived on had new houses going up. I walked down the street and talked my way into a carpenter's helper job. I learned what working hard was. Never carry just one framing stud, move fast, always look like you're working, and organize the job site, tools, and truck. I spent my days working hard and the nights smoking pot and watching TV.

That work eventually ended, and I moved on. I had found my dad; he had remarried and lived in Houston. His new wife, Kitty, had ten kids from her previous marriage and a lot of them still lived at home. Somehow, I ended up there. I think Kitty's kids mostly didn't like me there. I don't know if they liked my dad, but I landed there.

It was a good time for my dad and me. We connected on some level. My drug use was at a minimum, and he concealed his drinking well. He helped me get a hardship driver's license which allowed a fifteen-year-old to drive if they had to get back and forth from work or school and to drive them would be a true "hardship" on the family or parent. I got it the day I turned fifteen. I also got a job at the local Jack in the Box restaurant.

The house was close to our childhood home on Indigo. Strange, but memories drifted in and out from those days.

One of our favorite treats was a visit to a Jack in the Box. The mall near where we lived was still there and growing. I even went by the old house on occasion. It was so much smaller, older, and the big Chinaberry tree in the back was gone.

Eventually, I became a pretty good worker at the restaurant. I ended up working nights and sometimes I was the only one there. It was my first taste of real responsibility, and I enjoyed it. I remember one night I was alone working the "Box" when a guy walked up to the order window. He was an older, worn down looking guy with empty, wounded eyes. I stepped in front of the little window and asked him with a smile, "How can I help you, sir?"

He set a gun on the stainless steel counter between us and told me to give him all the money. I was shocked. What, was he robbing me? He was. I opened the drawer and took all the money, gift certificates, and anything else in there, put it in a bag, and gave it to him. As fast as it started, it was over. I called the police.

Looking back on it now, I was sad for that old guy. I wish I would have talked to him, tried to talk him out of it. I don't think he was there to hurt me; he was there to get money for food, maybe to get back into jail where he would be cared for—I don't know. The police caught him almost right away, and he went to jail.

My dad's neighborhood was an older established one with longtime families, and all the kids knew each other. I was an outsider on so many levels. But there was always the one common denominator I found I could use to get friends, drugs.

I began hanging out with the wrong crowd. I tried my best to seduce any girl who even bothered to look at me.

I felt so needy, and I lived a life in my mind that made no sense. I had agreed with satan's lies that I was not worthy; I was a loser. The slightest gesture from someone had me reeling with the thoughts, "She loves me; he hates me." In reality, I think those around me never gave it a thought.

The last thing I remember my dad doing for me there was to help me to get my driver's license. His drinking took him out again, and he left. I, of course, left too.

I realized I would need a car, but could not figure out how to save the money and still afford my drugs. One day it came to my mind that I could call my godfather. Being raised in a Catholic home, I had learned which traditions to follow.

My parents had asked the Fischers if they would be my godparents, and they had agreed. I was just a baby, but my parents and the Fischers must have been close. John had moved into the Houston area and taken a job working for Mr. Fischer in his auto supply store. I called Mr. Fischer and asked if he would loan me money. He did.

I made promises and guarantees I would repay him in an honorable fashion. I purchased a Firebird 400 for a thousand dollars, and never looked back. The car was never the blessing it was meant to be. I was dangerous when driving it; I did the minimum to care for it and misused it often. It would be twenty years before I made it right and paid Mr. Fischer back.

One night, I was side by side at a stoplight with one of the neighborhood kids. His car was fast, and he took care of it. I challenged him, and when the light went green, we took off. He led the way. As the block ended and we came closer to the next light, he slowed down, and I passed him wide open. The light turned red. I decided I would blow past and keep going through the red. I think at some point, I prayed I would make it. The chance of me killing someone was right in front of me. I can feel grief, shame, and disappointment today as I write this. I would not allow myself to stop. By the grace of God, I didn't kill anyone or myself.

I got to know some local kids and felt like I was a part of their community. Lauren was in our little group, and when my dad left, I knew I had to go too. I talked my way into her house. I don't know why her parents liked me. Most likely they felt sorry for me. Lauren's family was Jewish, and they practiced all the traditions. I remember one night I came home late from working and on the dining room table was a candleholder full of candles, still burning. I thought about it for a brief second, walked over, and blew them all out. It was a safety issue. The next morning, Lauren's dad explained what those candles meant. They were supposed to be burning; I think it was a Chanukah candle. I had no idea.

I drifted about for the next few years. I drove the Firebird into the ground and finally had to sell it. I found an old El Camino 454 on the side of the road and bought it. I drove that into the ground also. I got what I could out of it. To this day, I long for either of those cars back. Ugh!.

I was in my early twenties when I finally found a steady job at the local tobacco distribution center. I spent the nights loading candy and cigarettes onto delivery trucks for the next day's delivery. That is when I got to know Danny Dollahon.

Danny grew up in the area and knew everyone. Lots of girls liked him, and he liked that I knew where and how to get drugs. His parents got to know me and heard my lost boy story. They eventually let me stay in their extra bedroom. They should have checked my resume. This was a terrible decision.

Looking back, I have to believe his parents knew I was struggling with drugs. They cared about me, listened to me, and asked me questions. They asked how I was, if I had talked to my parents, or if I needed anything. It was one of the first times I had ever felt unconditional love from adults. They invited me in and loved me. My heart was moved. Although I continued to make really bad choices, the love they showed me was a light in my dark little world I so longed for.

The only true requirement from them for free lodging was attending church on Sunday. It was a given at their house. You went if you were there. It wasn't a battle to go; I did it to make sure I could keep my room at their house.

Their church was different than anything I had ever known. They went to a little Bible church. I didn't know what that was. The only thing I knew about a Bible was they were really big and sat on a table. Never opened, just a big, fancy, history kind of book.

It was the first time I had heard a preacher relate life issues and God together. People were talking about the Bible and stories inside the Bible. I saw people living in a way that was obviously because of all those things they read there, the things they heard on Sundays, and a desire from somewhere inside them.

Danny and I volunteered to help with the youth ministry on Sundays. We also met regularly with Terry. Terry seemed to care for us and shared what Jesus really meant and why He came. I am so grateful for God using Terry and Terry allowing God to use him. I was moved at that time to pray for Jesus in my heart and get baptized. I know on that day, that moment, Jesus was placing a marker, a stake in my heart He would collect on later.

I stayed with Danny and his parents for three or four months. In my heart, I knew it was only going to be a short season. Few things along my life trail moved me closer to Jesus than the time with the Dollahons. They modeled something I had never experienced.

Terry was not the youth pastor or an elder at that church. He was in his early 30's. He was a guy who knew Jesus and shared that with two young guys who needed what God offers. He gave me a Bible I have to this day, and in it is the date he gave it to me and "In Christ's love, Terry Moyer." It is a precious gift.

On a calendar, it was a short time—three or four pages, a handful of months. For my heart, the time with the Dollahons would be forever life-changing. Don't ever underestimate the impact on a life even when your time is limited. Terry and the Dollahons were intentional with showing me the unconditional love of Jesus, and it mattered.

13

The Law

The decision to use drugs and alcohol became harder after my time with the Dollahons. I did not stop using or living by the rules of the street. It was what I knew. Often, it seemed I used more to try to still the anxiety I felt inside. My heart is tender knowing now that it was God speaking to me. He wanted me to know Him, rest in Him, and to let Him care for me. I was not ready. Eventually, I became a driver at the cigar warehouse and would run my route each day delivering cigarettes and candy. One thing I also found was that if I threw an extra case of cartons of cigarettes on my truck, I could sell it for cash on my route for $70. I liked the extra cash, and it became a regular addition to my deliveries.

One afternoon I was driving back from my route, and I was stuck in traffic. It was creeping along, and I was impatiently waiting to get back to the shop. I saw a car nudge its way across the lanes of traffic to the right. People honked, and the driver struggled to squeeze by. From my viewpoint up higher than the cars, I could see it was an older gentleman and his wife. I slowly moved forward, and they were next to me on my right still trying to get through the traffic.

I think back on that moment often. That man was having a heart attack and fighting to get his car out of the way of others. His wife was desperate. People were so self-absorbed they honked and wouldn't let him in. If only I would have stopped. I can feel the wife's desperate emotions. I created a whole scenario in my mind. They were married for years, forty maybe. He was a veteran and solid to the core. He had grown children and grandchildren. He didn't make it through the night.

I can see that experience as clear as any I have—the fear on her face and the strength he had for her to get her out of the road. He was not going to die in the car with her stuck in the middle of the road. I want to cry as I write this. Sometimes, remembering things brings hurts from places inside me I don't understand.

Then one day, I was called into the offices at the warehouse. There was a lot of missing merchandise, and they wanted to know if I had anything to do with it. It seems they actually counted all the products as they came in and went out. They had boiled it down to my truck and my route. I was arrested and taken to jail.

I didn't have any way to pay a lawyer because I spent all my money on drugs. Somehow I was released on a self-bond and sent home. I never asked Danny's parents to help. I think they would have, but I just could not ask.

After the arrest, the drug use got worse as the pressure of everything became more real. I was in big trouble for the theft. I knew my time at Danny's was short, and I had to do something. It all came to a head one Sunday after church when Danny took a handful of pills before we left the house. We waited too long to get out the door, and we stumbled to the front door. His parents and their pastor and his wife were all sitting right there at the dinner table.

We slurred our goodbyes and fell through the door. His parents must have been horrified.

I needed to get a job, and somehow I got a position at a local apartment complex as an assistant maintenance man. I was a pretty good salesman. Clean clothes, a good smile, yes ma'am and yes sir. All those things go a long way. One job perk back in those days was if you worked at the apartments, you got a free apartment. Danny moved in soon after, and we set up shop.

I learned a lot in those days. I learned about the apartment industry and how to deal with people. I learned a lot of maintenance skills as well. I was taught how to paint and caulk and replace a light switch or disposal.

My court date came, and I was fined and put on probation for the theft. Even then our antics never slowed down much. The apartment was always a haven for girls. Danny and I had plenty of drugs. It never mattered how many drugs or which girl—I never felt happy or safe.

One day an assistant manager at the apartments pulled me aside and told me cops were on the roofs watching people in the apartments selling drugs. I didn't realize what she was saying. A few days later, someone was pounding on the door. The person would not identify themselves— then wham, wham, wham the door came down. The police stormed in.

We were having a party as usual. We did not have a lot of drugs out, but we were pretty high and had some girls over. The police forced us to the center of the living room floor. That was when they began a room by room search of the place. They destroyed the furniture, dismantled the apartment fixtures, and asked us time and time again where the dope was. They never found anything more than the small amount we had out on the table.

I was in jail for a couple of days before I was released again, on my own. The cops never found the big drug stash we had hidden, but someone else who knew broke into the apartments and found them. I only had a few days until I had to move out, and I had no idea what to do.

Insanity is defined as doing the same thing over and over again expecting different results. That was my life in a nutshell. For years, I was wandering, searching, and begging a God I did not understand to help me. I knew about Him and remembered the love I had felt once. I just did not know how to walk with Him, hear Him, or really believe in Him. I just kept believing everything turns to crap, right? No matter how good it may seem in the moment, it always turns to crap.

Somewhere along the way, a friend of a friend introduced me to a girl named Kelly. She was a cute, short, sandy-haired girl, who was younger than me, but loved to laugh and smoke pot. We started hanging out a lot. Her mom was a single mom who ran apartment complexes for management companies. She was really sharp. Kelly had her own apartment at a complex her mom managed and eventually, we moved in together. The laughter was short lived. Drugs, partying, fighting, and arguing were about the only things on the life menu.

Jackie, Kelly's mom, gave me a job as a maintenance man in the apartments. It wasn't long before Kelly announced she was pregnant. This was so not part of the plan—not that I had a plan—but I had no idea what to expect now.

Should we terminate the pregnancy? Go through with it? Get married? The pregnancy did not keep us from fighting. We were two unhealthy twenty-somethings trying to make adult decisions and fighting all the time. Eventually, I moved out and then back again.

Then God spoke. He told me I could not leave the baby. I had to stay close, be a man, and be a father to the child. No matter what, I had to be there. I don't know why I understood what He said and why it had such an impact on me, but it did. I suggested we go to the Justice of the Peace and get married. I knew in my heart this child could not be without his father's name. I was not doing it out of pride or arrogance; I truly felt the hand of God directing things.

I was there when Cody was born. The first time I saw him was surreal. I had something to do with that? I mean, I know how it happens, but I was confronted with the fact I am no longer living just for me. Amazing.

We were living together and tried to piece together what a home should look like. Kelly's mom was great at making sure Cody was cared for. She made sure he lacked for nothing and made sure I kept busy. We moved around following her mom's moves. Evans wanted to move back to Texas and came to stay with us. It was fine with me. My drug use continued and having Evans there would give me another excuse to keep using.

I remember one day when Cody was really little. I was up early on a Saturday morning. I am an early riser no matter what. I was sitting on the couch smoking pot when Cody came into the room and walked over to me as I stared at the television. He said a few words to me, waited, and then walked off. At that moment, I had an overwhelming conviction come over me. You mean you are sitting here stoned and missing the first things your son is saying to you? That was it; that is what I heard. My insides were crushed. I am failing at this thing. What in the world? Why is all this getting so hard? Kelly and I had decided to call it quits. She had had enough, and I was fine with her leaving. She moved out and lived with her mom. Evans and I were using more now than ever. I had no restrictions—just wide open drug use. I didn't know at the time Evans was tired of the drugs and was being convicted to make a change. I never missed a chance to see Cody, but the life I was living made it hard to manage in the chaos. He always had a way of looking at me, saying something simple that would convict me profoundly. My internal fight to be a good father, a good man, was at a breaking point.

Once away from the way we were living, Kelly began to get her life together. She backed away from the drug use and craziness. She called me early one Tuesday afternoon and told me about a twelve-step program for people with drug problems. She said I should go visit. What the hell was she talking about? She was the screwed up one. I knew what she was talking about. For the last several years, John had been calling me and asking if I had had enough. He was clean and sober now and knew I was hurting. When I told Evans about it, he said he had been thinking about it too. He was not happy and wanted a change. That night we went to the 7 p.m. meeting. It was Tuesday, April 17, 1986. That was the day I chose to do my best to not use drugs again.

Those were tough times but exactly what I needed. I found a family of friends in those meetings who cared about me and I could do life with. They taught me how to do things without drugs as the anchoring element. It was an amazing time for me. Many nights Cody sat in my lap through the meetings or played in the back on the floor. I volunteered for anything and everything. It did not matter.

The funny thing about the twelve-step program I was a part of was we were huggers. I think most twelve-step programs are hand shakers, but we hugged. I needed hugs. Even the big, burley ole biker dudes hugged the skinny little dudes like me. I loved this.

After being in the program for a while, I remember once I was at the airport. I was walking through the terminal when I heard someone call out my name. I walked over and greeted her with a big hug. "Hey, how are you? Where are you going?" It seemed she was taken aback a bit by my friendliness, but we exchanged pleasantries and trip details then said our goodbyes. As I walked away, I was thinking, "Who was that? What meeting did she go to?" At 30,000 feet I realized who it was. It was my insurance agent's secretary. She wasn't in the program as far as I knew; I really didn't even know her. Man, I bet her husband had a few questions. I still like to hug.

Kelly and I divorced with shared custody, and for the most part, we were civil to each other. I look back now and know her mom was a huge factor. I got a good job and a new place to live. At the time, it was the best job I had ever had. I was the maintenance supervisor over a large homeowner association. It was all coming together when I heard Kelly was moving to Austin. Her mom had moved there, and she was going to follow. Living in Houston, if I wanted Cody on my weekends and other days, I would have to drive three hours one way to pick him up.

I was angry, to say the least. I was just starting to get it together, and Kelly was once again throwing a wrench into it all. What could I do? I can't stop her. That was when God said, "Quit your job and move to Austin." Are you kidding me? Why would I do that? He told me I could not leave my four-year-old boy. I had to stay close, be a man, and be a father. No matter what, I had to be there. Oh man, he played the be-the-father card on me again. I gave my notice, packed my stuff, and moved to Austin.

14

A New Town and a New Life

Jackie offered me an apartment and work at her new Austin property. She was always trying her best to keep me in the picture with Cody. I got there and dove in. She let me wallpaper, put down floor tiles, fix balconies, and paint. I did anything I could, and she taught me the value of the work and how to bill her. I worked every day and night I could. She had a small side business back in Houston, and she let me take over the name in Austin: Etc. Services. It fit. I would do anything, and I made some money.

Cody began school and I loved it. During his time in preschool, elementary, and middle school, I was all in. I participated in after school programs, plays, reading time, PTA, and more. We spent every chance we could together. One weekend we went to the boat show and the next thing you know we owned a 15-foot Champion bass boat that matched our little Chevy Blazer. It was a rare holiday or weekend we did not fish. We traveled all over Texas learning to fish for bass. We did some crazy things during that learning process. Navigating storms, driving all night to a lake on the Texas and Mexico border, and crossing the international water into Mexico fishing waters and exploring. It was so good for us.

I continued my twelve-step meetings. I learned a lot volunteering under some extremely talented service workers. It is not unusual for an addict or alcoholic to be especially gifted, and I got to meet and learn from so many. They planned events and created marketing materials as outreach to the community. I went to regional, state, and world conferences. It was good for me, and they were a healthy family unit I relied on.

I dated a bit. Only once did it ever get serious. Helen was an amazing, beautiful blonde who was also deeply involved in the twelve-step program. We were inseparable for a period of time. I was learning about who I was as the fog from years of addiction rose. I was also seeing a therapist twice a week. Getting healthy was a lot of work. At some point though, Helen realized I was not the healthy choice for her. I had a lot of issues, and she needed to get free to heal herself. That was a hard one for me.

I dove into work, meetings, and of course Cody. We fished even more. My business grew. Jackie and her friends who worked at other apartment complexes and management companies would call and use Etc. I added a landscaping company once I figured out all my clients had lawn maintenance crews. I bid them, got them, bought a truck, trailer, and gear. Off we went.

My therapy included one individual meeting a week and one group session. It was so good for me. John, my therapist, was a small, dark-haired fellow about my age or maybe a bit older. John always dressed well, and I believe he really cared for me. One day when I went to see him, something was different about him. I sat down, and he sat in front of me instead of his usual chair to the side. He looked me in the eye and said, "I am sorry I have to tell you this. I have AIDS, and I am dying. I only have a short time left." I was devastated. John was my secret anchor. For four years, he was the one I relied on for direction and input.

It happened fast. John got sick and stopped meeting with clients, and one day, he was gone. I went to his funeral at the sculpture garden. I wore my starched jeans and button down. My boots were clean and almost shiny. Quite a few people were there, and I realized many were gay. I walked to the front of the room where there were photo albums and posters. I began to lose it. There was John in a dress, makeup, and feathers in full drag queen gear. I didn't know this John. That was not my John. I wandered back to my seat in a daze.

They held the service and asked if anyone wanted to speak. My heart raced as each speaker talked of gay pride events and trips. I had to get up and say something; I had to tell them who my John was. When one speaker quit, I jumped up, and without thinking too much, I walked up front. "That John in those pictures—that's not my John. That is not the guy who sat with me for years each week talking through my heart issues. That is not the John I knew." And then I walked out.

He had been very careful not to bring his lifestyle choice into our sessions. I so respected that man and even more so after realizing how much he cared for me and did not want to jeopardize our work in any way. Not that I would have been prejudice toward him being gay, I don't think I would have, but he just chose not to go there. John helped me a lot.

One day at work I got a call to bid a landscape maintenance project at an apartment complex in North Austin. I set a time to meet the manager. When I got into the office, I met with Sandra, the property manager. She was a striking young blonde and was all business. We walked the property and talked about her concerns. I made notes along the way. She gave me a date to have the bid back to her, and that was it. Or so I thought.

We got the project and began the work. My lead man was Wayne, a hard working guy with a smile. Everyone loved Wayne. He was great in the field with my clients, and he was especially effective with the ladies—not in an inappropriate way, but he knew how to handle the work, get things done, and be polite with a smile. When he found out Sandra was single and, of course, knew I was, he began taunting us both. "You two should meet," he would tell me every time he came back from her property. I was on a year's sabbatical and not committing to any relationships. We agreed to either attend together or meet at casual work and association social events.

We were the exact opposites in so many ways. She was a young, beautiful blonde girl who enjoyed nightlife and being single. I was a single dad who was interested in building a business and fishing with Cody. I had been hurt by girls, and frankly, I was enjoying time off from the idea of dating. She tells how she had never really thought about dating a single dad, a sober guy, and a guy who enjoyed being at home more than going out.

One day Wayne came back from Sandra's property and told me Cody and I were invited to a Hawaiian Luau at her property that Friday. I agreed to go thinking it would be a good client-relations move. The day before, Cody and I bought flowers from a flower shop and then made a hand-sewn lei. The next night we made our way up to the apartments to make a quick appearance and deliver her the lei. She was floored. It was a killer move on my part. I think if I lower the iron curtain a bit and be honest, it was spectacular because I wanted it to be. I wanted her to notice me a little bit more.

It wasn't long until my year off from dating was complete, and we began dating. It was fun, and I loved caring for her. I had bought my house and fully remodeled it by then. It was on the other side of town from her and to visit would be a big invite. When she finally agreed to come over to see where we lived, she tells of how when she pulled into the driveway and looked out over the open porch, green yard, and towering oaks and she thought to herself, "I could live here."

Our dating was defined by a couple of things, but none more important to me than being a seven year old's dad first. I would not pass on one of my nights, weekends, or holidays with Cody. Some she could be a part of, others it was just he and I. As much as that perplexed her, she honored it, and it set the stage for things to come.

What came was that we fell crazy in love. At one point, she went on a business trip, and when she left, we were mad at each other. I did something stupid I am sure. I sent a huge batch of flowers to her and a voicemail. I played our favorite George Strait song over the recording. I asked her to travel with me to meet my brother John in New Mexico.

We drove only back roads and visited the sights and attractions off the main roads. We finally made our way to a small ski lodge in the New Mexico mountains just opening for the fall season. Our room overlooked a flowing creek, and that night as we sat on the floor for a picnic in our room, I asked her to marry me. She jumped up and immediately called her mom. I am still waiting for her to say yes. Of course, a mere formality at this point—but waiting.

We planned our wedding and tied the knot. I remember sitting on the front row after all the pictures and ceremony. Everyone had gone downstairs to the reception except a couple of my buddies, and as I sat there, I realized okay, we would go on our cool honeymoon, come back in about ten days, and she will be moving into the house with Cody and me and won't be leaving.

Cody was eight when we married. Sandra loved taking care of us, and we loved her taking care of us. She loved the house since the first day she saw it and wanted a family and home of her own. We three were a great match.

Our kids came along directly. I used to introduce Sandra as the mother of my many kids to come. One day she asked me, "Exactly how many kids are you thinking?" It was a premonition of things to come we now laugh about. Cody came with the deal; we were a package. Taylor was our first, a girl. Then Jon-Michael. We chose not to know the sex of our kids before they popped out into our lives. I would say two things about this. One is you rarely get a surprise like this, a gift from God. It was so powerful. The second is I have never felt closer to God and His miraculous wonders than when my three kids were born.

Now, I did a few things wrong. I was so nervous I kept wiping Sandra's face with a wet washcloth to the point she yelled at me to stop. Maybe she was just grumpy, but I was probably a bit overzealous. I say if a woman wants the epidural spinal shot to cut the pain, then yes. Other than those things, men just enjoy the ride. You will never know love, full love, until you have a child of your own. As I write this, I have to admit to one thing, our first grandchild is on the way and from what I hear, putting up with your kids and all that goes with that is worth it when you get a grand-kid. That love exceeds even the love you have for your kids. So we are excited.

15

Business

During our courtship, Sandra and I devised an idea for a business and launched it just after we were married. It was a small directory (think Yellow Pages) for management companies and apartment managers. It included ads from all types of vendors they would use like painters, flooring, carpentry, and more. Sandra soon quit her apartment job and took over running the directory, *Vendors Round Up*.

She was so much a people person, and she flourished in the role. I gave her backup and was in charge of figuring out how to design, print, and distribute the directories. We worked from home mostly and as technology quickly moved forward, the process of printing and developing the materials became easier. For me, it was all self-taught and a huge learning curve, but I liked it.

Eventually, we hired Randy to do all the graphics for *Vendors Round Up*; it was too much for us. One day when we were sitting together, he suggested we start a country music magazine. It would be easy he said, and it is Austin, Texas. So we did. No, really that is how it happened, and with all we had going on with the construction business, the lawn maintenance business, and the *Vendors Roundup*, why wouldn't you add another project, *Country*

Line Magazine? And that doesn't include any family time or new babies on the way.

The country music magazine took us to places we could never have imagined. We went to tons of country music shows; we had to. There was a huge learning curve. Just making up a press badge does not get you behind the stage. A photographer can come in and take pictures during the first three songs but then has to leave—not stay in the back of the auditorium, but leave.

I wanted, of course, to write a story on Willie Nelson who lived near us. I met him one morning by chance at his studio, and he invited me on his bus to hear his latest reggae songs. Just he and I. He had it so loud there was no talking. We sat at a little table, and he smiled. He reached over and pulled out a wooden box, opened it, and rolled a joint. Then he lit it. When he offered it to me, I declined. It was weird to decline to smoke a joint with Willie in some ways, but I did. Really, I passed on it.

Once when Taylor was a baby and Sandra was breast-feeding, we had to go to a Garth Brooks concert. We did not take the baby but had to take a breast pump. It wasn't this huge contraption, but it wasn't a pocket size. They gave us a private suite so we would not miss the show, and Sandra could use her breast pump in private. True story.

I did a story on this new up-and-comer who was playing a concert in the Walmart parking lot; his name was Kenny Chesney. We sat on the back of his bus, and he talked about working out and golf. There may have been a hundred folks or so at his show that day. Today, he is the king of stadium concerts around the world.

Another time, I sat with George W. Bush when he was governor of Texas. We had a really cool conversation and I got great pictures with him. He eventually made it to the White House, and I was invited to a few presidential things when he would come back to Texas. Amazing. Sandra and I traveled all over the country invited by tourist companies to write about areas they were promoting. They paid for every detail. We could not believe people did this. Our kids benefited as well. I wrote travel and adventure pieces for the magazine on everything from surfing summer camps on the Texas coast to Yellowstone, Colorado ghost towns to Florida resorts. Crazy.

Long nights, long hours, the learning curve, and God were what made *Country Line* happen. We printed the magazine and distributed it all over Austin and the area every month for twenty years, and then online for another five or so.

The radio show was a spin-off from the *Country Line Magazine*. The local blowtorch FM country station wanted to partner with us in the magazine. It made perfect sense for both of us to work together. After a year or so, we talked about what we could be doing together. After we acknowledged the regular print for radio promotions, they asked the big question. So what else could we do, what would you like to do? I asked for a radio show. I had no real background except hanging out with their guys on air and at events. But I thought, well you asked. Just so happens the outdoor guy quit his Saturday morning spot the week before, and I wanted to do an outdoor show. They gave me one hour on Saturday mornings from 5 to 6 a.m. to talk about outdoors. So now we had a radio show.

Everything we ever did, we learned as we went. My favorite stories to write were outdoor stories. I was never a technical guy. I can't talk ballistics or current ecological importance of prairie grass. I was a storyteller and shared the parts and pieces of a fishing trip or hunt.

One of my best decisions was to join the Texas Outdoor Writers Association. That was a huge deal. I walked among true journalists and writers. I admire them for so many reasons. Just that I was accepted was astounding. My background did not match up exactly, but the members were very good to me. I had a lot to learn, and they gave freely. The men and women of that organization opened my eyes to what true journalism is. I will be forever grateful for their help.

Eventually, we sold off the landscape business. The following year Etc. had the best year ever; work was pouring in. But in December, God said stop. I somehow knew it was coming. I did not know exactly that it was God talking at the time, but it was so clear that was what I was to do. In worldly terms, it made no sense, and I would not recommend a guy reading this who has a successful job or business to just walk away from it unless you know for sure, and that is a tough one. I went out to the truck, took out my tools, and never looked back.

Vendors Round Up was similar. We had opened another issue in San Antonio, and it was doing really well. It was everything we could do to hire, manage, and be everywhere we needed to be. Sandra's heart was torn when she would have to leave the babies, and that pain was getting to be too much. We both knew leaving the kids with daycare was not what we were supposed to be doing. I was also listening to Dr. Laura on the radio, and she advocates for a family to make whatever cuts they must to have mom or dad at home to raise the kids. God spoke. Our competitors in the market offered to buy *Round Up*, so we sold it to them. It was time.

Looking back over the businesses God planted in our lives, I can see His strategies. From here at 30,000 feet above the past, it is clear. The landscape business introduced me to Sandra. The construction business supported our family and generated the funds to buy our home and the start of our life together as a married couple. I also learned a lot about operating a business, taxes, payroll, marketing, and dealing with customers.

Vendors Round Up taught us the publishing business and forced me to learn computer graphics and to write content. Then came *Country Line Magazine* and the doors it opened. I had a huge learning curve to join the world of journalism. One thing I was intentional about was building relationships. This is one place being a member of the Texas Outdoor Writers Association helped a lot. I began being published in other magazines and learning what that takes. I loved the radio show and the fun of telling stories verbally. Learning to interview and keep a conversation moving. Entertaining people on the air, live.

Looking at all of this, I have to admit, easily, that God did all this. There is no way in the human world a guy with my background—a middle school drug addict with all the brokenness and flaws—would achieve the successes I have had without Jesus. How do you go from all that to President of the Outdoor Writers Association? An award-winning writer and photography guy? The host of the number one outdoor radio show in Texas over and over? Only God.

Then to see the way He was preparing me for what He had for me in the future takes my breath away. He does that; He loves to do that.

16

The Neighborhood

Our little spread is about two acres on what was the edge of town. The city has since engulfed us over the years, but we have maintained our country living for now. The street is a dead end with about twenty houses, and everyone knows everyone. We know cars that don't belong and the cars of relatives and grown kids who come to visit on the street.

When I first came to Austin, I had an apartment for Cody and me. We were always upgrading our apartments too by adding cool fixtures, paint, and custom flooring. Lucky for me, the manager was my ex-mother-in-law, and she let me. One day God introduced me to an old fellow at the breakfast restaurant. He was a local realtor, and we small talked about the downturn and places around town for sale. I told him if he ever found a cool house that needed work, I would be interested. Months went by when out of the blue he called me. He had a house on the far south side of town going up for auction and would I be interested? I went and looked at it and thought to myself, there is no way.

The front yard was overgrown, and a large dump truck was parked in the middle of it. The house was an old 60's two-story, and everything was still 60's original. Fencing and posts crisscrossed the backyard as if they had farm animal pens. There was a garage and a falling down office building. To me, it was perfect. Problem was I had no idea if I could win a bid on something like this. I agreed to his plan and forgot about it. It was a week or so when he called, "You are a homeowner." Oh my gosh, what? Now what do I do?

At the time, pre-Sandra, Cody was six or so, and the construction company was in full swing. Anytime my guys or Cody and I had extra time, we went to the house and worked. The place began to turn into a home, and not long after, Cody and I moved in. I always had a driving heart to have a home of our own, a house. Now we had it. Our place. Our home.

We have always been the place where every kid on the block would end up. We had ponies, go-carts, dogs, and a trampoline. It was always a safe, cool place for kids. Angela, the little girl at the end of the street, found out we had a horse and I got my first ranch hand. Cody worked hard, but Angela loved it.

I am a guy's guy, and every boy on the block wanted to hang out at the house. I had knives, tools, BB guns, and archery gear. For whatever reason, there were always a couple of single moms on our street who had boys. Those boys always found their way to the house.

Across the street were large fields and an abandoned ranch the kids would explore. If they did not take the horse, they took the dog; if not the dog, then BB guns or a bow. We always offered the gear, and they were happy to accept. For all the outside projects I had from fence repair to roofing, I rallied the boys to help. The reward was usually a trip for pizza or burgers. Fire pits and backyard campouts were all open to the kids on the block—mostly the boys back then. They loved it as much as I did.

We lived in the house a couple years before Sandra joined us. Once she moved in, the house really became a home. A mother's touch, a woman's touch. To be honest, I had to really work on myself here because Cody and I and the neighborhood boys had gotten comfortable doing what we did. With the exception of Angela, who none of the boys would make the mistake of messing with, we guys peed off the porch and left stuff out. We wore dirty jeans and boots in the house and swept up later. We were really pretty clean for a bunch of dudes, but when Sandra came, things changed.

The laundry was washed, dishes were cleaned, and a regular routine was set for dinner time. We had to make sure we considered the things we wanted to do, because now we had another person as part of the team—TJ and Cody, Angela, and all the boys on the block. It wasn't long before Sandra had won everyone over, and the new norm set in. It was good.

One of the first boys I felt like I should spend time with lived a few houses down from the corner. Shawn's mom and dad were not married, and his dad did not give him the time of day. I had never mentored or thought about being a mentor. I had the time I spent in T.A.R.S., but that was it. For the most part, I just invited Shawn to do things with me. Sandra got to know his mom and really promoted the idea of me spending time with him. We did a little bit of stuff together; then one day he quit coming around.

One Saturday morning when I went into the shop storage closet in the back garage, I noticed something was different. What was all over everything? Oil? Slimy oil was splashed on everything in our storage closet. What the hell? It was a mess. I went in the house and asked Sandra what had happened, as if she would know, and of course, she did not.

So as I began cleaning it up, I remembered having taken Shawn back there to help me dig out some boxes. This was the act of a rebellious teen mad about something. I knew that because I had done things like this before. I marched down and pulled Shawn out of his house. He denied it, but I could tell it was him. I told him whatever I did, I was sorry—please don't do those kinds of things. Then it was over. I tried to handle it well, but I had zero training—just my heart and a bunch of fear. I heard later Shawn struggled most of his life with anger issues. When a dad causes anger in a boy, those things happen. A lot. A boy desperately needs a dad.

From almost the beginning of when we moved into the house, we had problems with one of our neighbors next to us. When they finally put their house up for sale, we prayed for a minivan and kids to move in. It was close. Jim and Marie bought it. Their kids were grown, but they had grandkids our kids' ages! Thank you, God.

Kyle, his sister Kayla, and their mom moved in with Jim and Marie after their father and husband was killed in a driving accident. Kyle and Kayla were close to the same age as our two youngest, four and five. We loved them immediately. The grass was worn down to a dirt trail between the two houses. They were the kind of kids who would just walk in the house without knocking. Our home was their home. Kyle, even to this day, will do it and head straight to the refrigerator. I love that. I knew we were going to love on those kids. It was not because we had a plan to be a mentor or preach to them. It just felt right, and we knew God was in it.

Kyle was the first kid I encountered who made me feel like the things we were doing might make a difference. We did everything together, and when his grandfather bailed on the family, we did even more. Kyle was all boy, and he hungered for everything. He worked hard and played hard. He never backed away from working with a post-hole digger or an ax.

You could tell Kyle's dad had made an impact on him. Boys who lose their dad reach for things to connect with them. One of Kyle's prize possessions was his dad's tackle box. There were lures, hooks, old bobbers, and fishing line. A mishmash to most, but it was a treasure trove for Kyle. He carried it any time we went fishing and used what he could. I never bothered to tell him a particular lure or set up would not work where we were fishing if it came from his dad's tackle box. It didn't matter; it was sacred.

Cody had begun his college years, and during those summers, he guided at the Y.O. Ranch in the heart of the Texas Hill Country. The ranch is a famous Texas ranch known for their hunting and cowboy events. He was a guide for clients of the ranch and youth hunting camps they held there each summer. We really enjoyed the time there and learned a lot about how a ranch and summer camp operates. Kyle loved that place, and Cody guided him there for his first kill—a black buck.

The neighborhood kids ebbed and flowed. As our kids grew, they brought over their friends, and everyone wanted to hang out at our house. Sandra was the Kool-Aid-mom and took the kids, any kid, to the parks, zoo, library, or events she read about. She was always planning activities. The comment I made years before, "This is Sandra, the future wife of my many children," began to become real. We just did not know they would not be all from us biologically.

17

A Church Family

I remember back as a young guy, sixteen or seventeen years old, hitchhiking to see my family. They were living in Birmingham, Alabama. I was still in Houston when I got on the road. It was dark as the clock hit 2 a.m., and my ride turned off the Interstate dropping me off at a random exit in lower Alabama.

I walked down to the side of the road and prepared to keep going. It was dark, and the traffic was really light. Long days on the road, trying to be a friendly person, trying to stay awake when riding with someone, and not having money or food will wear you out both mentally and physically. That night, standing there, I was exhausted, hungry, and lonely, and to top it off, it began to rain. I was all alone in the dark, crappy weather. Again, a kid out at night and feeling really lost.

I looked out across a freshly plowed field, and off in the distance, I saw a tiny little farmhouse with the front porch light on. I thought to myself in that desperate moment, "I wish I could just go over there, knock on the door, and ask them to take me in, care for me, and love me." I was almost broken. But alas, I decided to just stuff all those feelings. If I let them out, I would surely die right there; I couldn't.

Looking back now, I can see that God began to reveal to me where I would find that feeling of family and love. I found it in that little church that Danny's parents introduced me to. I found it briefly in the homes of other families who took me in off the street. I found it again in my twelve-step program.

Today, I find it in my church and my men's group. I dearly love these people. It is one of the biggest blessings that comes from a walk with Jesus. I am sad for folks who go it alone without a church family. God knew we needed the church.

First Corinthians 12:12-16 says, "For just as the body is one and has many members, and all the members of the body, though many, are one body, so it is with Christ. For in one Spirit we were all baptized into one body—Jews or Greeks, slaves or free—and all were made to drink of one Spirit. For the body does not consist of one member but of many. If the foot should say, 'Because I am not a hand, I do not belong to the body,' that would not make it any less a part of the body. And if the ear should say, 'Because I am not an eye, I do not belong to the body,' that would not make it any less a part of the body" (ESV).

Sandra and I were led to our first church as a couple by family and friends. We were married by one of the pastors there, and we were sold on that being our home church. We served in little things like setting up chairs or helping in the nursery. I learned in my twelve-step program early on that to be a part of something, you have to participate. The old timers in the meeting would say, "Get here early, set up chairs, stay after, and clean ashtrays." It was fun to get to know the people of our church. We both hungered for it, and we were willing to help, and every church needs help.

When John, my therapist, passed away, he had set up our group to transfer to another therapist. I was only there a week or two and knew God was calling me away. My new church offered ministry training, and I heard God say, "That is where I want you." So I left the group and committed to a nine-month training in the Stephen Ministry. Stephen Ministry teaches lay-people in a church how to effectively counsel those in need. I wasn't anyone special in my eyes. I was probably the last person for ministry training, but I went, and it was astounding. I loved the fellowship and feeling like I was part of something important.

I volunteered to start a twelve-step meeting at our church, a hybrid of Celebrate Recovery. I committed to one evening a week, and I would do my best to lead it well. It was a big commitment. We lived twenty miles from church and being there from 8 to 9 p.m. every Tuesday was a chore. But I really felt like it mattered. We had mild success. Some nights I sat alone and read, other nights we would have five or six.

I did this for a couple of years until I found out that staff was counseling drug and alcohol folks off the street and not referring them to our group. I asked them about it, but they just never got it. I was a trained, hard-line twelve-stepper. You don't just give addicts things to help them, because most of the time they are working you. You have them go to meetings, meet some standards, and work their way through the recovery process.

This didn't sit well with me. I felt I had worked hard and was trained to help. It was really hard on me and ultimately the reason I felt it was time to leave. We loved our pastor; he married us. Sandra went to Israel with the church and was re-baptized in the Jordan River by our pastor. We did everything we could to help there. It was our first church and life changing.

The other thing was since our kids were getting older, we felt it was important for them to have church friends they would see at school and closer to our house where they could gather. Getting them to youth group and activities forty-five minutes one-way if there was no traffic was getting to be a lot. If we found a good church close by, then they could do church life and be at all the youth functions.

Sandra was out of town one week when I packed the kids up on Sunday and headed out to find another church. Just a mile or two down the road we saw a sign, Fellowship Bible Church, and it pointed to the high school. I turned in and parked. There were a lot of folks walking in so we fell in. As we entered, a greeter who must have recognized us as newcomers asked me, "Are you all new to Fellowship?" "Yes, we are. Can you guide us?" He walked us around, told us about the church, and walked us to the kids' area. "Okay, you two (Jon-Michael and Taylor), adios," I said with a smile. They walked right into the area for their age group, and my host walked me into the auditorium.

Service was good, really good. The pastor was younger and carried a great message. The worship team was killer too. I really liked after the service as the band played and folks left, the lead guitarist cranked a few riffs. I have to say, for me, for the most part, it was good. When Sandra came back and we all went together, it was an easy sell. The kids recognized school friends and attended weekday events. It felt so good to have a new church family and new friends.

One Sunday, we were sitting in our regular seats, front row left. From there we could see the behind-the-stage curtain. As the band played, I noticed our pastor walk up. He was behind the stage, and no one could see him except us. I saw him get on his knees and begin praying. It was intense; it was real. I could see him wipe his eyes when he was finishing. A man who was weeping over the message he was going to bring. I was moved beyond my understanding. My standards for pastors went way up that day.

I participated in a men's group in those early days. It was Wednesday mornings, led by a strong former military leader, and the study was pure Bible knowledge. It was good teaching for some; for me, it was really hard to sit still and pay attention. I felt I was being talked to. I have never learned well that way. Now tell me a life story, tell me how your brokenness affected you and how Jesus came in—and I will be engaged. Heck, even better, shed a tear in brokenness, and let's get real. The men's group eventually disbanded.

Those first few years at Fellowship were so good. We loved our family there. Sandra and I led a home Bible study, did service on Sunday, and went to and served at every function. Then one day I heard the pastor would be leaving. It would be another season God used to train, guide, and teach us. It would remain our church, and we would begin to pray for the next pastor God had for our church family.

Jody Mayes came to Fellowship from Denver, Colorado. He and his wife moved to Austin to be near their Austin grandkids. Jody had been a pastor in Denver for years at a big church. He did not come to Austin to preach or be a pastor; he came to be a grandpa. He came to the new men's bible study and all of our men's events. When our little church hit hard times, he agreed to step in and help a little. Well, the search for a new pastor never landed a new pastor, and eventually, Jody was tapped to fill in permanently. You know the ole church trick, "Just fill in for a day, a week, forever."

At the time, I was doing outdoor activities with the boys in the neighborhood and a few from church. We called it Country Line Outdoor Ministries after our magazine in the early years. Then we changed the name to Kids Outdoor Zone and KOZ to fit the outdoor radio show, The Outdoor Zone.

I also found a book I had no idea would change the way I felt about this walk I was trying to have with Jesus. *Wild at Heart* by John Eldredge was a game changer. I can't say for sure where it came from or who gave it to me, but it answered so many questions. I remember asking Sandra to please listen to it on a trip she was making. She tells how she wept as she listened. "Now, I understand; I get it," was her comment to me on the phone while she had pulled over crying.

That led me to explore more about John Eldredge and his ministry, Ransomed Heart Ministries. Now, I had been moved to tears by the Holy Spirit plenty of times. He was exposing my heart to me in all kinds of ways, and I was all in. But this was different.

When I saw that Eldredge hosted a four-day "Boot Camp" in Colorado, I signed up. It is a lottery because so many want to go. I finally got in and went. It rocked my world.

I came face-to-face with my heart, Jesus, and so many things became clear to me. My disclaimer here is there are a lot of ways to access your heart. Jesus can and will use all types of ministries, trainings, and conferences. I can't define what He will use for any guy—that is up to God. But I can say this was what I needed, and it was so good.

When I got back, things became clearer to me on my mission. Jody and I became closer, and I started calling him by his given name as a boy back in West Texas, Joe Don Flack—Joe Don for short. Joe Don had started the Wednesday morning Bible study back up, and I started calling "BS" on the teaching. "I call BS. All that stuff you are telling us, all the information you are giving us is great information. But explain to me how, when I drive out of here this morning, when I turn onto the highway, how will this work in my day today? Tell me how to do this from my heart. Teach me to operate from my heart." Joe Don liked it, and the other guys started questioning things. Our Wednesday morning men's Bible study came to life. Not just because of me, but because we began going after our hearts. It was good. Really good.

Eldredge talks about how every man wants questions answered. Do I matter? Deep inside, guys want to know who they are. They want to do something that makes a difference. They want to be a part of a battle for good. They want to draw from the depths of the male foundation. For most of us, we have been wounded along the way, and it keeps us from coming alive. We are told from early on to be a good little boy, sit still, and behave. Then as men, we are told to do our duty, help stack chairs in church, and pass the plate. We were to sit still and be a good man when deep inside we wanted to jump up, run around, explore the mountains, hunt, and fish. If our fathers had abandoned us physically or emotionally, we longed to know the things he never taught us. Were we initiated into manhood? How do we do this parenting thing, this work thing, and this marriage thing? Why am I so restless? Why don't I truly feel alive in my walk with Jesus? This is where I found myself. It was a lot, but it felt so good to finally get my questions answered. God was moving.

Sunday Morning

People were shuffling all around that Sunday morning as I stood in the hallway. The director of children's ministries came rushing up to me. "TJ, the teacher for third to fifth grade boys did not show up; can you come fill in?" I was not expecting this. Rumor has it this is a well-used tool by directors of Sunday school classes to lure folks into teaching a class. I fell for it. How hard can it be? Turns out I really liked it.

I continued to be there every Sunday for the boys in my class (the trick by the director worked—note "my class"). The problem I had was the curriculum. Now, this was powerful stuff. It had all the bells and whistles. You got an email the week before your Sunday. When you got to church, there was a folder and papers in it. Any felt animals, crayons, and colored paper were all included if needed. I kid about the felt animals and crayons, but the materials were expensive and well done. I just could not connect the dots in my head.

I would take the virtue and Scripture and march the boys outside. There I would make up hunting and fishing stories and include the virtue and Scripture in the story. It was funny when moms would stop me in the halls and say, "I am not sure how bear hunting fits into Sunday school, but my son loves your class." The classes grew to be the biggest in the Sunday school. Boys brought their friends and neighbors. I had to recruit my buddies off the back rows of the church to help me with all the boys, and they loved the time with them too. It was not your usual Sunday school class.

Then one Sunday, we came up with an idea. What if we invited the boys to meet us at the pond down the street next Saturday morning for a couple of hours and teach them how to fish? We announced it in a pretty informal way to the boys and their parents as they picked them up. That next Saturday we were inundated with boys. They came in droves and brought all their friends. Wow! As time went on, we thought we could do more things like this. So we planned hikes and survival skill days.

We realized the single moms were relying on us to mentor their boys, to be an example to them. Of course, we were teaching them things about being honorable and good young men, but it was becoming more than that. I got intentional with Scripture and virtues. We didn't beat them over the head with it, but we would sit them down and talk for a while at some point during the Saturday. It was a boy's level of teaching in the way I was looking for at my men's group. What is real life? Tell me what you did to overcome something in real life when you were a kid or a man, and how God fits in that.

We were doing something here, and it mattered. I know it is not a conventional way to mentor boys about Jesus, but it fit me, it fit us. What if we took them hunting or fishing for a few days on a ranch somewhere? There was so much I felt led to do. The idea kept growing, and I just could not let it go.

18

Stepping Outside

I was inspired by the Y.O. Ranch experiences and by a friend of mine who held summer and fall hunting camps for kids. Mike Marbauch leads Christian Outdoor Alliance and finds ranches that let him bring kids out for weekend and week-long hunting camps. When we talked, he encouraged me to do the same and offered any info he had to help us.

My first run at it was with a group of older boys, early high school. We went for a weekend to a friend's place that offered hog hunting. I was the only leader, and I remember so clearly sitting there by the fire that first night thinking, "How do I start a conversation about what is going on with these guys?" I fumbled around a bit. Thank God these boys and I had a little history and the weekend turned out fine. No major spiritual breakthroughs for them, but for me, I was on a mission. I wanted to learn how to talk with the boys and how to get a fireside heart conversation to happen.

The idea of the camps grew. I recruited guys, and we did other outings with the boys. It was a really good time for me, and I loved the boys and time with my friends. Of course, I have a thousand stories.

Once when we were on the coast, a hurricane came in, and we had to leave in the middle of the night as the roads were flooding. Boys fell off things and got banged up. I learned a lot about what not to do too. Letting boys shave their heads from losing a bet makes Mom unhappy when you bring her boy home. Cut out sugar for the boys. Don't try to live off Red Bulls and coffee. Give the boys chores, so you don't have to do everything. Huge learning curves.

We didn't always kill stuff or include hunting. As a matter of fact, that was the lesser of the camps and outings. Yes, we advocated it and if possible included it, but it was not required to get inside the boys' hearts, to get their attention. They just wanted to be with us. They longed for guy time, and the woods were their solace. To give you an idea of some of our time together, I have included one of my blog posts from our website:

Survival Camp (Blog Post)

With Kids Outdoor Zone youth adventure ministry, Jesus has and still does come alongside us time and time again. He loves on us and cares for us. He carries the yoke we struggle with and talks to us in those still, quiet moments, encouraging us and comforting us.

Over the last few months, we have learned to "press in," to strive for God's love and direction in our lives. We are learning a lot about preparing our hearts and our intentions before acting on behalf of Him. He showed us this weekend that He is there and He loves that we love Him and are coming to Him for cover and direction.

This Friday, we left Austin with eight boys, one guide-in-training, and three men who have a heart for the Lord and boys.

Saturday was spent teaching survival skills to the boys as if they were stranded from a plane wreck. They learned about finding and purifying water. They were taught how to start a fire and create an SOS. They built debris huts and learned how to select the right spot to build shelter. They caught fish with survival tools and ate them. They all did a great job.

We love all the guy activities. It gets hot, we get tired and hungry, but we bond together during these lessons. This trip was no different than ones we have done in the past, except that in the weeks leading up to this trip, our leaders, prayer warriors, and intercessors cried out for Jesus to be with us, to heal the boys who were coming, and to love on them. We wanted Jesus to show us how to love them, care for them, and lead them to Him.

Saturday evening started off tense with a lot of the boys tired and hot. That can be fuel for anger, frustration, and a mean spirit. The talk around the campfire was all but loving and caring. One leader called for a time of quiet reflection and for all the boys to separate for a time. They were not allowed to talk or be together. They spread out in the pasture, valley, and creekside.

When they returned, we pressed in. We talked about where they were in their walk with the Lord. That is when He came. The Holy Spirit filled the valley, the pasture, the campground, the area around the campfire, and the boys. Over the next period of time, they shared their hearts and heartbreaks, their love for family, and worries. We wept and hugged and cried more. This was one of the most powerful times with God many of us had ever experienced. The wounded began healing, and the lost accepted His direction and caring. Eternal, life-changing moments flowed from the ten-year-old to the seventeen-year-old. By the end of the time together, we were exhausted, and sleep came easily.

Sunday morning was beautiful, and a cool breeze crossed the valley. We awoke to find the Lord was not finished with us. One young man with a wounded eye from months before woke in severe discomfort. His eye was red and swollen, and he could not keep it open. A leader asked if he could pray healing over him, and as he did, the Lord told him to press in. He prayed over and over and over as the boy's eye got better and better, and then, like the man on the road to Jericho, his eye healed. Healed. A physical healing. A wounded eye from a wounded boy crying for the Lord to help him, heal him, and be with him. It was nothing less than miraculous. I have never experienced this before and don't usually pray like that, but it was so good, so real, and so pure.

After breakfast, the boys made their way to the creek. The cool waters were a comfort in the heat of the day Saturday. This Sunday morning they became a place of healing and commitment to live a life for the Lord. Four boys accepted the eternal gift of life with our Lord in front of their peers. The time was joyous and filled with cheering and laughter. A true day of glory for the Lord.

The blind man took up his garments and followed Jesus after he was healed. Lord, we pray these boys, mentors, and leaders hunger to follow You each moment. It was not a prayer that Jesus prayed that healed the man; it was the blind man's trust in the Lord that healed him. Lord, thank You for the boys who inspired faith this weekend. Thank You for their hearts of innocence and joy. Thank You for filling us with the Holy Spirit and His guidance. Lord, thank You for those who covered us in prayer and stand beside us when we waver or feel down. Holy Spirit, use us, tool our hearts into servant hearts that please You.

The survival skills for the boys at this camp were well received. The one boy who had done Marine Corps training summer camp said it was awesome, and he learned a lot. As far as we leaders, we changed the name from Survival Camp to God Camp. He provided the boys with survival tools they can use for eternity, and He used the leaders along the way. We, again, found He provides us with pure, fresh living water; burning fire; comforting, safe shelter; and food for life. He provides the best survival tools we could ever need, and no devastating crash required.

The camps inspired us, and all the time we spent doing a once-a-month Saturday get-together at my house, the park, or somewhere to keep the guys together, God was building something.

19

Validation
and Quiet Places

By this time, we had been publishing the magazine and cranking out the live radio show for years. The construction company and the *Vendors Round Up* were both gone. I had joined the Texas Outdoor Writers Association and had become active in their events, committees, and Board of Directors. I was writing for our publication and had the opportunity to write for national and regional magazines and newspapers.

During this time, I had met a corporate officer from a large regional outdoor retailer. We became friends and over time did a few projects together. This was not unusual since being a writer and radio guy got me in the door places I would never have imagined. I learned as I went.

One day as I talked with my friend at the retailer, he mentioned they were opening a new department at their corporate headquarters in Houston, and I should consider applying for a position. The department was Outdoor Media. The idea was that their expansion into other states and other outdoor retailers coming into Texas required them to step up their game. Their advertising and marketing departments were making serious mistakes when it came to the outdoors.

One example I saw was a huge interstate billboard depicting a couple of guys duck hunting. They were situated in a duck blind with one guy, a nice camo shotgun, and a retriever, and the other guy with a scoped deer rifle. Oh my, a deer rifle on a duck hunt. Yeah, they needed help. I applied the best I could. I had no college and no real high school education. Generally, my resume for a corporate job seemed pretty weak. He was a good friend, and he would put in a good word for me. I got an interview.

On the day of the interview, I drove the two hours to the national headquarters and sat in the parking lot watching people walk in and out. They were for the most part well dressed in office attire, and all had lanyards with nametags. Could I really be one of them? It wasn't my ego; it was a total life change. It was a really strange thought.

The interview went well. The guy who was hired to head up the department seemed fair and was a highly educated and connected outdoor guy from Alabama. I liked him. Several weeks went by, and I had really forgotten about the corporate job idea and moved on. Then the call came. I was offered the job.

Sandra and I both agreed it was a gift from God, and I should do it. We would have all the benefits we never thought possible—health care, retirement, and vacation. We could move to the best part of Houston with great schools, maybe build a new home. We would put our home on the market and see what God would do.

I had really bottled up my emotions here in a lot of ways. This call and job were more than all the benefits and opportunities I read and thought about. It was so much more. I hit my knees and wept. I don't understand, Jesus. How can You possibly find this junior high school educated, drug addict, broken kid, and raise him up to a job like this?

I was no longer those things in Christ's eyes, but deep inside, the battle was there. I had made agreements with the devil that that was who I was and breaking those agreements was tough. God and I were chipping away at it, but it was a lot, and I held onto it for a very long time. He was validating me, telling me I was worthy, I mattered, and I was not those things. He showed me a lot by giving me my own cubical.

I turned over my duties at church and said my goodbyes to the men in the men's group. I also said bye to our home Bible study family. I gave up my coaching positions with the kids' teams and everything else I was a part of. I was moving on; we were moving, and that had to be a part of it.

The drive was about two hours, and I would leave on Sunday evening and stay until work was over on Friday. Some weeks I was traveling and would not be home. It was both exciting and lonely. I met some top outdoor people in the industry, like television personalities and manufacturers. I got to participate in projects that I would see roll out in the store and think, hey, I did that.

One of the best things I did was write the television scripts for their outdoor show. I had never written a television script, but hey, how hard can it be? It was tedious, but for some crazy reason, I liked it a lot. I would add in ideas for them to capture on camera, what to say during the show, and of course, script out the commercials. A couple of times I got to actually be there when they filmed. That wasn't so great because they sure didn't like somebody telling them how to do what they did. I had done a television show of my own for a couple of years by then. It was an outdoor hunting and fishing show with Texas country music stars. So I knew what I was trying to get on camera was good, but these guys had had a sugar-stick sweet deal for years that nobody ever questioned, so they didn't care for me. My people-pleaser side was really bothered by it. My TJ side thought they were jerks. But I still loved the scripting, and I learned a lot from it.

I rented a room in a home with a couple of other guys. They were good young men and loved to watch baseball and drink beer. No problem; I just wasn't interested. I love baseball but didn't drink. So I would retreat to my room and write. My guys from church wanted to keep meeting with the boys one Saturday a month, so I would script out what a Saturday would look like. Then, when the Saturday came, they had a plan. If I was there, it was great, and no matter what, we had a plan. There were times I wasn't there, and they would call me after the boys had left to tell me how great the Saturday was and how the boys had loved it. I found myself retreating to my room or the hotel rooms when I was traveling and writing out exactly what and why we did this with the boys. I was drawn into getting it done, so when I left my church, the guys would have everything they needed to keep going with it.

Putting our house up for sale was surreal. I couldn't imagine selling it, but then I was becoming detached from Austin. Some weekends Sandra and the kids would come to Houston, and we would look for houses and places we would like to explore in our new area. It should have been fun, but it never seemed to be that exciting. Finding a home like we had was going to be hard, and the new company wasn't going to be pitching in. I also checked out a few churches. I was spoiled with feeling a part of my old church. I visited all kinds and sizes, and I think tried really hard to fit in, but alas, I wasn't with my family, and that just made it feel unofficial and half-hearted.

I got to know some folks at work. I liked them. My favorites were the ladies who ran the kitchen. In this giant corporate complex, our offices sat right next to the cafeteria and the Hispanic ladies who ran it were super sweet. Every day at about 10 a.m. they would take a break from their cooking and have their lunch. I would wander in and get a cup of coffee and joke with them. I started bringing in deer sausage after I got to know them. They would cook it up, and I would join them for an early lunch. It was a win-win. Upper management never cared for my early lunch breaks with the help, but I didn't know it at the time.

Eleven months and five days into the job, I was let go. There was a lot of turmoil in upper management, and apparently, BS rolls downhill. I had a lot of questions for Jesus. Really, Jesus? You brought me here. You gave me this job. I have been away from my family for almost a year. My house is for sale. Why would you do this to me? I cried again as I drove to my little room I rented down the street from the office. How would I explain any of this to anyone? Shame and those little agreements swept over me again. I packed my belongings into my truck. I backed out of the driveway for the last time. I headed back to Austin.

An interesting tidbit: I had heard Jesus the weekend before. He told me to pack all the extra stuff I had and to take it to Austin. I had collected a bunch of things there in my little room. To take it back to Austin did not seem to make sense. I had no idea there was a pending problem. I had no idea that God's plan included me leaving the job and moving back the next week. I could not have carried everything in one load. He knew.

When I got back to Austin, I called my mentor, Jimmy. He and I had met several times while I was at the new job that year. When I came to Austin, I would try to meet with him. He was a dear friend and the next morning at 5:00 a.m. we met, and I asked him point blank, "Why would Jesus do this? Why would He take me away from everything I know, my kids, my wife, and isolate me for almost a year?" I was pissed, and I wanted an answer. Jimmy sat there a moment over his eggs and then said very matter-of-factly, "TJ, God had you there for a reason. You have to ask Him what that was about. He will answer you, but you will have to talk with Him." Oh great, I am so not in the mood to talk with God after He did this. I hated Jimmy's answer, but I knew it was right.

20

Re-Entry

Now that I was back, I re-entered into the life I had left. God was watching out for us in one way I know for sure. In that almost full year I was gone and our house was on the market, two people looked at it. The market had crashed, and apparently, there was no interest. So okay. God, I will give you that one. I started back into my men's group and church on Sunday. When it got around that I was back, some friends who lived in the area called and asked me about the outdoor program the guys at my church were doing. They asked if they could start one at their church. That's when God revealed to me why I had been sent to Houston.

I am a busy guy. I say yes to things more often than no. Yes, I will do setup at church; yes, I will help with that meeting; yes, I will coach; yes, I will meet with you; yes, I will take some boys hunting. I realized God had taken me away from all my busyness to put me in a still, quiet place in that bedroom to write out the outdoor program in detail.

God had downloaded an eighty-page manual on how to do a Saturday with the boys. A training manual for the guys who wanted to do KOZ. God used the television script writing to teach me how to structure a Saturday activity. He also gave me the KOZ prayer, sit spots, and other keys elements of what a Saturday should be. I had it all written out.

Then He said to give it away to any man in any church who wants it. What? He said if my guys and I could do this in one church, how many boys could we rescue in two churches, twenty, or one hundred? The key element was more guys in more churches going after more boys. God spoke.

I must give credit to my dear brothers who stood by the boys and the program on those Saturdays I was not there. They met and kept it alive while God was developing the details. I will be forever grateful for their hearts for the boys and Jesus. They are a big part of why KOZ exists today.

I needed to do a few things, and the first was to go see my pastor, Joe Don, and get his input. He knew the passion I had for the hearts of the fatherless boys. He knew the impact we were having on boys, their moms, and their families in our church. He knew too well how badly boys need good men in their lives.

Joe Don's dad was a West Texas oilfield worker. A guy's guy. A man's man. One morning when he was three-years-old, his dad was going to take him fishing. What a treat for a boy, time with dad fishing. For some reason, that morning his mom said no he would not be going with his dad. That broke his little heart. He cried as he watched his daddy load the truck and drive away. It was a just a few miles down the road Joe Don's father swerved to avoid a sheep in the road, went into a ditch, and flipped over. His dad was severely injured and died a few days later from his injuries. For a young boy to lose the most important man in his life was painful. Questions that required a dad's answer did not get answered. His mom remarried, and her new husband gave Joe Don his name, Mayes. Joe Don Mayes, Jody for short. His stepfather was a drinking man. As hard as he tried, Joe Don could never get his stepfather to acknowledge him. For him, he was fatherless, and his heart was wounded.

Joe Don also knows the heart of a fatherless boy and how the outdoors can soothe the hurts, and if you added a man who would love on a boy, care about him, and mentor him, then together they could move mountains. I told him about the idea of Kids Outdoor Zone, KOZ, and how God told me to give it to churches everywhere. He looked at me a minute, smiled, and said, "Okay, how can I help?"

He and Jimmy became my first KOZ Board Members. I assembled others and pursued a nonprofit status, a 501c3. God brought in Steve Hall who was with the Texas Parks and Wildlife Department and a close friend. I asked two other close and dear friends who knew me. Alan Magraw, who was soon to be mayor of Round Rock, Texas, and Dr. Buck Vantrese, a vet and very close personal friend. Dr. Buck got the 501c3 done.

The next thing was to train the guys around us who wanted the program. These guys were anxious to get groups going in their churches and get the materials. I rallied them and asked them to bring a few key guys to help them on their Saturdays. I trained them up and launched them. The program worked at their church just as it had at ours. It was amazing to see it happening.

I remember going to the meetings and seeing boys and men I did not know. I thought how crazy is this? They would use the KOZ prayer and do sit spots and all the KOZ things we do. To top it off, I would hear about boys asking Jesus into their hearts and men who were transformed by the experiences with the boys. I was blown away by the whole thing. To this day, it almost feels unreal when I get emails, texts, and see Facebook posts with guys doing KOZ.

The prayer became more real. Lord, how do You want me to share this program with other men? How do I let every man in every church that might want it to know about it? I tried a few calls to friends who were outdoor journalists, and we had a few articles written in papers around the country, but very little came from it. I tried reaching out to other pastors in our area, but about all I got was crickets. Then the call from Hollywood came, and I thought okay God, You are going to blow this out of the water.

"Mr. TJ Greaney," the caller asked. "Yes, it is," I replied. "I am with a production company in Hollywood, California. We produce Mike Rowes program 'Dirty Jobs,'" she went on. "I found you and your son Cody here on the internet and see you do a lot of outdoor things, hunting, fishing, etc." "Yes ma'am, we do." "Well we are considering a new reality program, and we would love to talk with you two about the idea. We think you would be a great fit for the show." Now this idea to spread the program of KOZ had never come to mind. A reality television show with millions of viewers. God, You always blow my mind! This is of course what He would do. All I have to do is wear a KOZ shirt, a KOZ hat, mention KOZ during the show and "bam," the fire is lit.

Cody and I talked about it and, of course, Sandra too. We agreed that as long as we did not have to take off our clothes or do stupid things that would degrade or violate our faith, we would do it. We would just have to see what the show was all about, and to do that we had to fly to Los Angeles. They were paying for everything, and I thought, if the worst thing happens, then I still get to do this with Cody, and it is a story we can tell for years to come.

We arrived at the airport and were chauffeured to our hotel. Over the next few days, we did interviews and video tests. They said they loved us and, of course, Cody and I were just having fun. They gave us very little information on the show except it would have an entrepreneurial twist to it, and we would compete with others. Sounded right up our alley. After a few days, they sent us home and told us contracts would follow. Three weeks later they did. We had an entertainment attorney look them over. We were sure we were going to be a pretty big deal and needed to protect our interests.

We returned the contracts and waited for details of when and where we would be going. I practiced my signature—or autograph I guess it would be from now on. After a month or two, we just returned to our lives and forgot about the show. Then we got the call. "Mr. Greaney, we love you and your son, really we do. We are sorry, but we are going to go in another direction right now, but we will get back with you." It wasn't long until a new reality show was announced about duck hunters in Louisiana. What a ridiculous idea for a show. That thing will never make it. What were they thinking?

Okay, God, what was that? Why would You do that? That made no sense. It would have been a great way to showcase KOZ and get the name out there to millions and millions of folks. I was dumbfounded. It seemed the kind of thing God did in my life, totally out of the blue and beyond anything I could imagine. So now I guess I just sit and wait. Pray. What the heck, Jesus?

21

Kicking Off God's Plan

I love seeing the heart of a boy light up when he figures out he can do something. Our mantra in KOZ is "Do Hard Things." It fits so well on so many days with the boys. This whole idea to share KOZ with any man in any church was getting confusing. I knew it was what God had said but not sure what it all meant.

My local home group, the original KOZ group, needed men leaders and that was when I recruited Don "Beefsteak" Discoe. Don was new at church, but he was a guy's guy and looking for a mission. We became fast friends. Don is a leader, creative, and a hard worker who hates doing anything less than 100 percent. I invited him to join us one Saturday, and he will tell you I just kept giving him more to do. He did the training and never looked back.

Don's addition to our group was a shot in the arm for us all. It wasn't long before he began doing something incredible. Each month he would bring boys from his neighborhood. First one or two, then three or four, then six or seven. It was amazing, and his love for the boys didn't end at noon after KOZ. It was all week if he saw one of the boys. When he would pull up after work, they would ride their bikes up his driveway and meet him as he got out of his truck. This was KOZ in its purest and finest form. Don's input created program tools as it grew.

We had built a small website for the ministry, and it got a little interest. One day I received a call from a guy in West Virginia. Pastor Dan Cook had been looking for a program for his church and asked if he could use KOZ. He explained he was an outdoorsman and that his church was small, but he thought hunting and fishing would interest his men and draw in boys from the community. He also said he would like to go hog hunting in Texas. How could this get any better? He came down, did a little hog hunting, and then I trained him. He went back to West Virginia, and that was that.

A couple of months later Pastor Dan called me. "I wanted to tell you something amazing," he began. "I have more boys and men coming to my KOZ Saturdays than I do to church on Sundays. I have guys from other churches bringing boys." Wow! I don't know what I was expecting, but this was perfect. It validated the idea that this program could be duplicated and operated from other towns and states. So the prayers continued. What does this mean, Jesus?

A few weeks later I was sitting in bed checking my social media before I turned off the lights and went to bed. It is imperative, of course, to make sure you check all that stuff before bed in case somebody posts a funny picture. Pastor Cook posted that he was taking his men from his church to the Wildfire Conference for Men in Lynchburg, Virginia. Ten thousand men would be there, and the speakers were Duck Dynasty—the show that would never make it—Tim Tebow, Joe White, and other great Christian speakers. It would be a men's conference like I had never heard of before. God said, "Call them, and ask them if they need another speaker." What, are you crazy, God? I am not a speaker and could never compete with these guys. He kept it up as I sat there in bed. "Call them." I negotiated it down to an email, and I sent it to the conference email before I went to bed.

It was first thing in the morning when I got an email back. Yes, we would love to have you. Sorry, all our keynote speakers are filled, but we would love to have you come to do two workshops on starting a youth hunting and fishing ministry in a church. Well, okay then, I accepted and began the process of what the heck I was going to do. I needed flyers, a banner, and a few shirts or vests or something with KOZ on them. Holy cow, what did this mean? I asked Joe Don and Don if they would go with me, and both said yes, to my relief. But it was up to me to plan this and figure out what this was going to be.

One thing I did was to look through the list of other workshop speakers and see if I could get information from them on what to expect. I had never done a workshop, and this was going to be a big deal. Don had a lot of experience, and I had done sales, but I hoped I could meet with someone before the event and just learn from them. I emailed every other presenter I could find information on. There were dozens over two days presenting all different types of things—outdoors, cars, motorcycles, and more. Guy stuff at its finest.

We arrived in Lynchburg a couple of days early and found our hotel. The event was at Liberty University, which I knew nothing about. I was amazed to learn about the college, its history, and Thomas Road Baptist Church. Oh, my gosh, this was ground zero for so many Christian organizations and leaders. Dr. Tim Clinton was the mastermind behind the Wildfire Conference, and he knows men's ministry. He founded the Association of Christian Counselors and many other faith-based missions. Of course, God knew where He was bringing us, and you could feel His presence.

Only one other presenter replied to my emails and agreed to meet with me. When we talked, he told me he only had a few minutes, but he would be there. I was excited to get the inside scoop. Rick Magee was the Executive Pastor for Hyland Heights Baptist Church just outside Lynchburg. It was a big Baptist church, and he also led the outdoor men's ministry there. We met in the lobby the morning before the event, and he explained how the seminars worked and what his outdoor ministry was about. He told me how they had a large piece of property for events and hunting. Honestly, I was jealous.

Joe Don and I told him about KOZ, the history, and how it was rescuing boys. It was hours later when he finally said he had to go. A single mom had a broken toilet, and he had the replacement in his truck. "They are probably getting desperate for me to get there," he laughed. Rick said after he left our meeting, he thought to himself, "I can't not do this program."

The next morning, we showed up at the convention arena ready to set up. We were directed to our spot which was in a parking lot next to the tractor display and outdoor gear store. Well, this isn't what we were ready for. We didn't have a pop-up tent or tables. Then God said, "Go inside and ask if they have a little table you can use inside the arena." "Well I guess we do, let's see what we can do," was the answer. They gave us a table on the same level as all the other inside vendors. We stretched out our banner, laid out our flyers, and waited to see how it would go.

The weekend went by quickly. It seemed as soon as we started, it was over. I really enjoyed talking with all the guys, and the seminars went well too. One thing I learned from the Ransomed Heart guys was to use video and movie clips. I included a couple in my PowerPoint presentation. That weekend we had over 150 guys sign cards asking for more information to start a group at their church. I went back a couple of weeks later and did my first training tour. I had never done anything like it, but it seemed natural. God surely connected the dots, and at the end of the four weeks, six churches were trained, including Rick and men from his church.

As I think back, I really had no idea what to expect from this trip. I had never heard of the Wildfire Conference, Dr. Tim Clinton, or even really thought about going to men's conferences to let them know about KOZ. I had always thought it was just going to be the media in general, like a television piece, a story in a newspaper or maybe a magazine. I suppose had I sat down and strategically thought about where and who might be interested in KOZ, I might have realized it, but I don't tend to be that kind of thinker usually. God rescues me there all the time.

I tried to talk to pastors. I figured they would be the guys who would love the program, love my enthusiasm, and listen to my pitch. Then they would take it on, rally a group of men, and make it happen. I learned differently. Joe Don told me pastors get hit on all the time, some several times a week. Everybody has the newest, greatest, and best way to do kid's ministry, women's ministry, small groups, and the list goes on. What he doesn't need is another chore or homework. We do have pastors bring the ministry into their church, and the ones who believe in it and lead a group of men into it from their church have seen big returns.

One of my favorite things is when a pastor listens to one of his men who found KOZ at an event. Then he listens to his guy(s) and supports their heart's desire. Not every pastor or church will do this. I get calls from guys with broken hearts because they get turned down or their pastor has his plan, and KOZ does not fit. I get it, a pastor is the CEO and must have a vision for his church. I know some guys are just not ready to take on something like KOZ, and the pastor knows the men better than we do. It can be a muddy and uneven trail for a guy. Jesus has got to be in it.

22

Mentors and Canada

So the next thing was to find men's events around the country and see if I could get in. The best scenario was to have a break-out session or speaking part and a table. Sometimes I just got a table, but I took it. Meeting the leadership at the events was the key so that I could maybe build on the relationships and our presence.

I thought for a while I should be invited to keynote some events. Heck, I was leading KOZ. But God humbled me here. When I met the top speakers who were up on the big stage, I realized I just needed to be where God had me. They were incredible speakers, pastors, and storytellers. I needed to share what I know best, KOZ. It was where I knew myself and God's mission for me.

What did happen as KOZ grew and I was invited to be a part of more conferences was who God introduced me to. I found out about the National Coalition of Men's Ministries and started going to their events. I met Robert Lewis there. Robert is one of the longtime leaders of men's ministry and "boys to men" ministries and also wrote *Raising a Modern Day Knight*, *Men's Fraternity*, and other cornerstone leadership and training books for men and boys. He is such an encourager and has met with me every time I asked for counsel. His materials and the way he presents them were how I based the filming efforts for the KOZ video trainings.

One of my biggest life change experiences in my walk with Jesus was after reading *Wild at Heart* and going to a Wild at Heart Boot Camp in Colorado. John Eldredge penned *Wild at Heart* and a dozen other titles that have been so important to me, and when I asked if he would meet with me, he agreed. We have become friends, and his team at Ransomed Heart—Morgan Snyder, Bart Hansen, and all the others—has been instrumental in our execution and desire to really hear God leading in all we do.

I met Stephen Kendrick, the Christian movie producer, at the Fatherhood Co-Mission events and he too has been open and available to us. Stephen is so passionate, and every time I leave from a visit with him, I am fired up and ready to do more—to do my best for Jesus.

The point is that God introduced us to these folks as He rolled out KOZ, and I see His hands on every piece of it. It was all His timing, His plan.

I found a lot of conferences and got traction on getting invites. Some were good, some were great, and some not so great. As my calendar populated with events and guys who wanted to start groups in their churches, I got really busy. It was not unusual to spend a week going from an event to training to another event. I didn't want to turn anyone away. My Southwest Airlines miles stacked up.

At this point, Rick Magee and I had become really close. He was a guy I could trust, and he and I shared a lot of the same life lessons growing up. One day God revealed a thought to me that I shared with him. "What if you came to work with me in KOZ?" I didn't know exactly if we could afford it or if he would even be willing, but I had to find a solid guy to help me, and one on the east coast would be perfect. In God's perfect way, He spoke to Rick and cleared a trail for him to follow. It was scary for us both. With the cut in pay he would have to take, his wife would have to go back to work. Could we actually keep a long distance relationship going in ministry? Could I give up some responsibilities and decision making? I knew one thing for sure: I could not do this alone and grow it in a healthy way. Then God released it, and Rick came on board. We both knew every step was anointed.

Rick is an administrative guy. He does numbers and budgets and planning—the stuff God did not include on my gifted side of the list. He is a huge people person and knows Jesus and his Bible. One of the hiring agreements was for him to go to a Wild at Heart Boot Camp, and that helped get us on the same page in a lot of areas. He was already a solid Robert Lewis, Men's Fraternity guy, and that was one thing he brought to the table from his side. It is always so much better when God orchestrates the way to the solution.

We started sharing the conferences and training. Twice the manpower brought in twice the responses, and it grew. Learning about conferences, where they are, and who might be there has been a learning curve. One in the Los Angeles area Rick went to was pretty funny. He set up our normal table with deer skins, hunting gear, our banner, and a slide show with lots of hunting and dead animal pictures. It is us! As the men rolled in and walked by, he felt resistance. In conversations, he heard things like "We don't hunt much here." Halfway into the conference, he changed the look of the booth and talked about camping, hiking, and fishing. When he called me after the event, he told me it was not exactly our demographic. We laughed, not at the guys, but we learned that the culture of who we are wouldn't fit at every church or in every community. Interesting revelation.

Both of us found ourselves in a wide-open mode with speaking, booth shows, and training. Our group count grew from ten to twenty to thirty trained churches. It was April of 2017 when I realized I had air-miles expiring if I did not use them. I jumped online and looked for a men's conference, the farthest one away I could. There was one in Coquitlam, BC. I called them, and they offered a table. I booked my flight and went. It was cool to be out of the country, and I thought, KOZ is now international. It was almost surreal to be in Canada. I used my passport at the huge Alberta Airport with no problems. I remember eating at a restaurant one night; I wanted to eat local foods but did not know what that would be. I went alone and sat next to a couple eating seafood. I ordered the same. We began a casual conversation, and it eventually turned to who are you and why are you in Canada. That was when it got funny and weird both.

In Canada, as they explained, folks don't have guns. They didn't need them and thought Americans—especially Texans—were crazy for wanting them. They told me their oldest daughter was going to college in Denver and their biggest fear was she might be influenced by someone with a gun. Maybe even want to buy one. I asked them what they thought of pot. They said it was not a real concern for them. I asked if their daughter smoked pot at school with all the legal pot smoking going on in Denver. They did not think so, but it did not worry them; heck, they said, it would be legal in Canada soon. I said, "So you are okay with your daughter smoking pot but not learning to shoot a gun?" They said "yes." Where was I, and how the heck would this play out in Canada?

The conference was great, and I met a lot of really good guys. There were plenty of fishermen and hunters. Most guys didn't have a stockpile of guns, very few handguns, but lots of hunters with rifles. I collected names and made it back home. It was an amazing trip.

Several months went by, and I got a call from a men's ministry pastor who had met me, and KOZ had been taking up a lot of space in his thoughts. He finally had approached the leadership at his church with the idea, and they said to do it. When he called, he wanted to set a date for a training.

Tom and his church are in Abbotsford, British Columbia, just across the border. I was so excited. We were really going to be international if they started a group. Tom is a very detail-oriented guy, and he must have called a dozen times with questions. As we planned it, I thought this might be a fun trip to do with Sandra. My idea was to fly into Seattle, make a leisurely drive up along the coast, and cross the border near Abbotsford. Rick and I love taking our wives with us when we can. They are relatively easy to travel with, many times fly free because we travel so much, and are great roommates. They lead the wives' training the night before the men train, and the women in the churches love to see them.

For me, Tom had it set. I would come to speak at the Saturday men's breakfast, which would be packed, and add a little last minute recruiting for our training. Saturday night he had planned a wonderful dinner with the wives, and then after church Sunday, I could have lunch with the pastors. Monday we would meet with the guys and train them up. Again, Tom was a planner. He was ready for me to come.

As it sometimes does, life got in the way of my ideas, and Sandra could not make the trip. I kept my original itinerary and flew into Seattle. There were no hassles with the rental car and taking it into Canada. The drive through Settle was slow, but I made my way north. My GPS brought me right to the Canada border crossing. I pulled up a little apprehensively; I had my passport and everything in order, but still felt a bit intimidated. I think you are supposed to. When it was my turn, the border guard asked a few questions then handed me a colored piece of paper and told me to park and go inside. Well, okay I guess. I had never done this before, not north anyway.

I went inside the building. It was a vast open area with hard sterile floors and a bank of raised teller-style counters across the back. There sitting up high behind the counters overlooking all they could see were a group of young border patrol agents. One waved me over. I gave him my colored card and my passport. I expected to get a few quick questions and then released to find my way to the church. He asked me why I was there, who I was going to see, and what I was going to do. He logged something into his computer, asked me a few more questions, and then told me to go have a seat. Okay.

Over the next thirty or forty-five minutes, he was looking at his computer, looking up at me, waving other guys over and asking them questions, and pointing to his computer monitor. Honestly, I was getting mad. I felt like he was jacking with me. Finally, he called me back up and asked me about my criminal history. I told him I had nothing in the last forty years or more. He wanted details. I tried to remember. What in the world could he be worried about? Then he announced. "I am denying you passage into Canada. Please collect your things; the agent will turn you around." He handed me a printed slip with my passport, and I walked out to my car. They waved me through to the American guards. Those guys asked if everything was good. I said, "Yes sir." They waved me through.

I was in shock. I was doing everything I could not to blow up in anger and scream, and then I cried. I just fell deep into a dark place. I pulled over into a small church parking lot. It was a deep hurt I was feeling. I was worthless. Finally, the world figured me out. I was a poser, an imposter. That troubled, drug addict, school dropout kid was exposed. What would I do now? I thought, okay then, screw Canada. I will drive back to Seattle, catch the next flight home, and be done with this crap. I had had enough.

23

Holding on to Truth

I was devastated and had to pull over after coming back into the good ol' US of A. I tried to call Sandra, no answer. I tried Joe Don, no answer there either. Then I tried to call Cody, "Hey Dad, you make it?" I cried as I talked. He listened. I had to process it and get it out. I will say it here and a hundred more times, you have got to have men in your life you can lean on when times are tough. As I talked, God revealed what He wanted me to do. I would not rush home; I would not give up. Satan was at work, and we were going to stay in this a bit longer. I needed that time with Cody.

So I would stay in the area. I was told by the Canadian Border patrol not to attempt to hop to another entry point and try entry, or they would arrest me. No problem there, I was not coming over. I looked on the map and saw that Abbotsford was just down from where I was and just right on the border. On the American side was a small town called Sumas. I drove along the small farm roads to Sumas. When I got there, it seemed a lot of the town had died off, but I was praying, "Lord, please help me find a hotel room for tonight." I finally found a hamburger restaurant with a few hotel rooms above it. They had one room available. I took it.

Now I had to call Tom and tell him about the problem. It was really quiet on the other end of the phone as I explained my problem. My heart was full of shame and disappointment. I had no idea until later how crushed he was as he listened. He had spent a whole lot of time planning all the pieces of the training. He told me later he asked himself, "Why did you even try to do this? You should have left this whole thing alone."

As we talked, God revealed His next move. "Tom," I said. "What if I made a video and sent it to you? You could play it over the video gear for the guys. I will explain everything and then speak to them about KOZ and all I had for them anyway. It would just be a video." It was quiet on the other end. "Okay, I guess we can try that." I told him I would post it on YouTube for him that night, and we could talk early the next morning. I would put my phone on the desk, plug in my wired microphone, and just let God speak, and that's what I did.

God downloaded a thirty-seven-minute video, first take. No editing, no glamour. The audio and video from my phone were great. I had done some videos before, so I knew it would play over a big screen. I opened our KOZ YouTube and tried to upload it. The wifi was terrible, and I was up all night refreshing and trying to get it loaded for him. Finally, at about 4 a.m. I texted Tom and told him it would not load. He was up; he could not sleep either. I think back now how hard it must have been for him after investing in this guy from Texas. We agreed he would come across the border and get a thumb drive with the video on it. I never watched it all; he never watched it before he played it that morning.

He told me later it was one of the most powerful Saturday men's groups they ever had. The guys were stuck to the screen watching and some were even in tears.

As the video ended, they tried to have me call in over a video call live so I could answer questions. My phone and the program we tried did not work. It was just as we were going to blow off the idea when it popped up on my phone. They could see and hear me, and I could see and hear them. Guys asked questions and told me how much it meant to talk with me. We talked for twenty minutes before closing in prayer.

The next night the hotel did not have a room available. I found a church just down the street having a garage sale and bought blankets. I stopped at the store for food and water and drove up into the mountains to find a place to camp overnight. God led me to the most beautiful campground on a lake. I camped and hiked and thought about how amazing God was. I was overwhelmed with His love for me.

Over the next few days, everyone I needed to meet with came across the border. We set up a lunch with the pastors, and I shared with them the vision. The hamburger restaurant let me use an empty room they had with a table and chairs, and I brought the television down from my room each day to play the videos. The wives' dinner and the training went flawlessly. All of them walked across the border and back home to Canada. After it was all said and done, we knew God had connected the dots. Satan was hard at it, but he did not win. They launched their KOZ group a few months later, and it is flourishing. I will never forget what God did, only Him.

There are so many of these stories. The ministry continues to thrive. Groups are starting all over the United States and Canada. The video training is being used to ready the men, and their response is powerful. God is empowering so many men to do ministry at a level they never expected or thought they were qualified for.

It just boggles my mind that this little ministry is doing what it is doing. I am in awe when I flip through social media and see posts with boys doing outdoor activities in KOZ groups. For the most part, I don't know the boys or many of the men. But there they are, posed next to their first deer, with a fish, or sitting by a campfire. The KOZ men commenting on the post, "Jesus came to KOZ around the campfire." "Little Bobby got his first deer." "Johnny accepted Christ and was baptized in the creek today." They are teaching boys about giving back, hiking, survival, how to treat their mom, or how to change a flat tire.

God spoke to us again when we realized we could only train a few guys a year if we were doing it ourselves. He told us to create an online video training. With the help of our mentors and an extremely talented group of young video producers and editors in Rome, Georgia, we got it done after almost two years and lots and lots of elbow grease. It's His program and His tools.

I pray God continues the rescue mission of KOZ. I pray we find a thousand men on a thousand hills with a lamp for the fatherless. I pray these men mount up and rescue the boys.

24

Circling Back Around

My birthday had just passed; it was year thirteen for me. The family had finally broken apart, and I was alone. How does that happen? Why would that be my lot in life? I was an angry young man for a long, long time. I did not know how to do life. I blamed my parents, society, and anyone else who did not help me when I said I needed it.

A boy needs help navigating the trails of life he is to manage. My questions were ancient ones asked by every boy before and after me. I was not expecting anything a boy does not need or long for. I just wanted to know what to do and how to do it. I wanted to be loved and cared for. I needed to know my heavenly Father to give everything a center point. Habakkuk 1:2 says, "How long Lord must I call for help but you do not listen?" (NIV).

Dad was at home when I was little, and I got a piece of him. There were days I watched Dad build things with his hands. I got to touch and play with the tools. I explored the screws, nails, and bolts in the cigar box cabinet he built. I was fascinated by it all. The smell of his DNA wafted over us on those days. It is not that I remember him teaching me to hold a hammer or use a miter saw, but he was there, and we were looking over his shoulder soaking it in. The go-cart he built was released full throttle with my older brother in the seat. The rockets we launched were fabricated and set off under his supervision. The camping gear trailer with all its cubbies, corners, and pockets were intricate pieces of wood glued, nailed, and placed on a carpenter's pencil line that marked where they were to go. The level bubble wavering to center. The smell of fresh cut pine lumber and the feel of a well-hit nail driven into the wood. I was there to experience it, if only for a short time.

It was those handcrafted moments in time with Dad that I see God used to help me find work and fund my young life. I always looked up to the men who hired me as a helper on construction sites. They were so powerful in my life. I wanted to please them and make them proud. I worked hard without complaining. I showed up for work when I was told. God used all of these men, the long hot days, smashed fingers, and sunburned shoulders to craft my life skill. I was not a trained or skilled craftsman when I walked on a job site in the early days, but I was not afraid of it either.

Camping is one of my favorite outdoor adventures. Add the mountains, and you have my full attention. I long for the sound of pine sticks popping and crackling on the campfire. I adore the smell of bacon and coffee cooking over the camp stove. A cool breeze coming off the mountain. It's all so good for my soul. I long for it from a place deep inside.

The elk antlers stacked high at the mountain lodge. The sound of the fresh, cold-water creeks coming down the mountain next to our tent. The bear, deer, and chipmunks wandering through the campsites. The scar on my knee from falling down the rocks, I know now is called scree. Even the smell of the canvas we used as a tarp and tent. That is why I love the outdoors, the national parks, mountain trails, and campsites. There are nights when I can open the window near my bed and feel the cool air on my face. Just a slight breeze coming in gives me comfort. I know it is from those outdoor days as a boy. My senses spurring emotions molded around them.

I only remember that one race in elementary school. One time around. The one comment from the coach standing at the end and it affects me to this day. "You almost broke the school record," will forever stick in my mind. I almost did it. I ran well, but I could have done better. Mixed messages and thoughts surface even now when I am running almost every day on trails through the park. I like it. I can do it. Running seems to fit me. I am not fast; I would never win a race, but I run. Today, it is a marker from my past—memories as a boy.

Baseball is the one organized sport I love. I love the big park, green grass, and the signs around the outfield. I don't watch it hour after hour on television like my buddy John does, but a good day at the park is a good day period.

I was a good baseball player; at least I think I was. I had a natural ability at some minor level that got me high fives and "Good job, Tom" from coaches. I can't tell you my coaches' names. It may have been one game or ten. Somewhere I loved it and felt acknowledged and appreciated. Validated. A piece of my heart is baseball.

Mom was a homemaker when we were little. We enjoyed her fresh baked cookies, fried pork chops, and homemade mashed potatoes. We also ate iconic rural favorites like store-bought white bread, with pure cane white sugar and milk over it for cereal. Old school. Mom sewed, crafted, and decorated on a shoestring budget. I remember the large jar of buttons she always had. I remember the ironing board out, the sewing machine, and wood floors she hand waxed. She wore an apron, and we sat at the table for dinner. I love wooden cooking spoons, tin measuring cups, and wooden handle spatulas. I love family at home with food and laughter more than just about anything. I would skip the biggest party with the most famous celebrities and extravagant décor for a night with the family at home having dinner and watching a movie. Those things seem real to me. Honest. The way things should be.

For years, my family wavered and split. The cracks separated my parents from my life and the questions I had. I thought nobody cared about me and what I was doing. It took a toll. Skipping school anytime I wanted and never studying or being asked about my school work left me without perimeter fences. No matter how bad it got, the school moved me forward and left me to myself.

My life was wandering the streets, not having a home, and no money for food or a dime for a phone call. Walking fields of tall weeds in the cold and rain. No boy, no kid, should have to wonder where they will sleep at night, feeling alone and scared of the dark, and not having a safe place to call home. These are pieces of my heart that move me to this day. I see boys today who don't have a safe home, wandering about in life, trying to get answers to the questions, and my heart breaks.

The hurts, fear, brokenness, and lies are all places Jesus has come into my life and shown me I am not alone—those do not define me. He came for me. God uses this history to minister to boys who are walking this trail. Matthew 10:30-31 says, "And even the very hairs of your head are all numbered. So don't be afraid; you are worth more than many sparrows."

I had bad people who preyed on me. Without God's divine protection and Mom's prayers, it could have been much worse. The evil one manifests himself in so many ways. He is evil and pain. Kids on the street are not safe. There are even kids in a home who are not safe, are not loved, and are longing for the answers to the questions. Yet, those charged with caring for them neglect them.

Matthew 18:12-14 "What do you think? If a man owns a hundred sheep, and one of them wanders away, will he not leave the ninety-nine on the hills and go to look for the one that wandered off? And if he finds it, truly I tell you, he is happier about that one sheep than about the ninety-nine that did not wander off. In the same way your Father in heaven is not willing that any of these little ones should perish."

Sandra has said it before, and it is true. It is a good thing we don't own a farm in the country. If so, I would have renovated the barn into a dorm room and rescued every kid I could get my hands on. I know what that feels like not having a home, and it breaks my heart not being able to just grab them and care for them. I had good people who cared for me and helped me along the way as a boy on the street. They were God markers that kept me alive, taught me good, and trained me with no evil expectation.

The short story I wrote in elementary school was a marker. I see now where God used it to affirm me as a writer. The popular boy who did a lousy job reading my story was a marker. I decided that day that nobody would tell my stories. I tell stories live on the radio every week. God has made it clear that He wants me to tell my stories, and right now it's on FM radio and podcasts.

The brown-eyed girl could not answer the questions that the boy had. God knows I tried for a long time to let the girl in my life at any given moment answer the questions I had. It was not a verbal question but a constant internal question: "Do I have what it takes as a man?"

I searched long and hard to get those answers; all boys do. Many men are still looking. I got parts and pieces on construction sites and in a church classroom. The longing continued for so many years.

My heart returns to where it was loved and felt loved. It remembers the validation and experiences I had along the trail. I can look back now and see all the tender places God used to make me who I am. Even the smallest high five and "Good job." The five-dollar first prize and the wooden kitchen spoons. Those are the reasons I love the mountains, writing, running, wood construction, and family.

I don't want to lose the good for the sake of anger, pride, or pain. I want to learn to forgive and take the things God has for me from every situation. He does that, but only when we allow ourselves to be open to it. We have to be listening. We have to obey. We have the choice to make.

I could have never imagined forgiving my dad if God had not been there with me. My brother spoke God's words to me, and God gave me the peace behind it. God relieved me from the weight of the guilt I felt from all the things I did for so long. So many wounded souls, broken promises, broken hearts, and broken pieces are on the trail behind me. I hurt so many. Some I am afraid have died because of my influences back years ago, and I am so, so sorry.

If I don't walk in His grace, I can easily drop off the main trail into a dark place. My thoughts can wander into places the evil one knows well and will use against me. The evil one knows me well. I have to know my Father in heaven owns me, and I am His son, His child—His.

I am on the verge of tears as I write this. God rescued me; He came for me. Now I want to be a part of His mission. I am renewed, restored, and validated. I want to rescue the boys who need me.

Luke 8:15 says, "But the seed on good soil stands for those with a noble and good heart, who hear the word, retain it, and by persevering produce a crop."

I give full credit to God for every piece of the Kids Outdoor Zone ministry and how it happened, how it works, and how it helps. I see now He used the brokenness, the hurts, and longing in my heart as a boy and young man for His good. Of course, He would take all that and turn it into ministry. He would train me to write and give me a passion for the outdoors, a love for lost boys, and a hunger for fellowship with men of like mind. He did that from all those places I felt less than, unworthy, and lost. He took the agreements I had made, the anger, and formed them into His works.

He wrote the manual and showed me how to write the curriculum. He provided the KOZ prayer, the logo, and the idea. His details are so pointed. He focused me on one paragraph from a 450-page secular book that fostered the concept of the KOZ Sit Spot. A Sit Spot is a short period of time on a KOZ Saturday where the boys sit alone in the outdoors and write something the leaders can be praying for them about until they meet again. One small paragraph in a whole book, and He uses it today to connect boys' hearts to Him. So simple and so perfect. He has done all of KOZ that way.

If you had asked me years ago what I thought my future had in store, I would have said a good job as an apartment maintenance man or carpenter somewhere. I would have never thought of ministry. How could that be possible? Why would God even consider me? I had no idea what God could do. I would have put myself and God in a small box I could manage myself, as I always did.

Luke 9:23-25 says, "Then he said to them all: 'Whoever wants to be my disciple must deny themselves and take up their cross daily and follow me. For whoever wants to save their life will lose it, but whoever loses their life for me will save it. What good is it for someone to gain the whole world, and yet lose or forfeit their very self?'"

A legacy is not always the plan; it can be an act of God. My friend Lee's idea to listen to God at 11:11 was a gift from God. He uses it today to remind me of the joy of friendship

Lee brought. He uses it to jog my memory of the mighty power He shares in such simple things. God trains us for His work through our life experiences and a longing in our heart. All of us. You. He chooses you. Ask Him today, what is it Lord You have for me? Then do it, because life must be an adventure of mighty consequences.

"Regulators, Mount Up."

KOZ PRAYER
Lord, thank You for making us strong
and fierce warriors for You.
We hunt, we fish, and we share
our faith with others.
God bless our country, Amen.

References, Resources, and Heart Materials

The Bible

Wild at Heart, John Eldredge

Courageous, Sherwood Pictures, Kendrick's Brother Films

Raising a Modern Day Knight, Men's Fraternity, Robert Lewis

Coyote's Guide to Connecting with Nature, Jon Young, Ellen Hass, Evan McGowen

The Cowboys, John Wayne, Warner Brothers Films

Fatherless Scriptures

Train up a child in the way he should go, and
when he is old, he will not depart from it.

PROVERBS 22:6

He defends the cause of the fatherless and the widow, and
loves the foreigners residing among you, giving them food
and clothing.

DEUTERONOMY 10:18

And rejoice before the LORD your God at the place he will
choose as a dwelling for his Name—you, your sons and
daughters, your male and female servants, the Levites in
your towns, and the foreigners, the fatherless and the widows living among you.

DEUTERONOMY 16:11

When you are harvesting in your field and you overlook a
sheaf, do not go back to get it. Leave it for the foreigner, the
fatherless and the widow, so that the LORD your God may
bless you in all the work of your hands.

DEUTERONOMY 24:19

"Cursed is anyone who withholds justice from the foreigner, the fatherless or the widow." Then all the people
shall say, "Amen!"

DEUTERONOMY 27:19

...because I rescued the poor who cried for help, and the fatherless who had none to assist them.

JOB 29:12

A father to the fatherless, a defender of widows, is God in his holy dwelling.

PSALM 68:5

...learn to do right! Seek justice, encourage the oppressed. Defend the cause of the fatherless, plead the case of the widow.

ISAIAH 1:17

This is what the LORD says: Do what is just and right. Rescue from the hands of their oppressors those who have been robbed. Do no wrong or violence to the foreigner, the fatherless or the widow, and do not shed innocent blood in this place.

JEREMIAH 22:3

"So I will come to put you on trial. I will be quick to testify against sorcerers, adulterers and perjurers, against those who defraud laborers of their wages, who oppress the widows and the fatherless, and deprive the foreigners among you of justice, but do not fear me," says the LORD Almighty.

MALACHI 3:5

Religion that is pure and undefiled before God the Father is this: to visit orphans and widows in their affliction, and to keep oneself unstained from the world.

JAMES 1:27

Acknowledgments

Today, for me, the hurts and offenses I experienced as a boy have faded. I remember the good over the bad. I am grateful for that. We can spend our lives bound by those things. I see now they are the distractions that steal our joy. Jesus gave me a gift and I know it. It produced for me a new life, one I could never imagine. I tell folks if I had written my idea of the best life I could imagine 20 or 30 years ago, it would have fallen far short of what Jesus had planned for me. I pray my story will allow others to release their hurts and ask Jesus into their hearts. To follow Him and find the life they long for inside.

To acknowledge everyone who has navigated this trail with me would be impossible. There are those of you who in one word, one cup of coffee or chat around a campfire placed a marker in my heart that changed me for the better. Thank you.

To Mom who prayed when that was all that was left. Today I see that as the greatest gift you could have given me. I think God hears moms' and dads' prayers for their kids a little over the others He gets. To my little brother and sisters, I don't assume to know the hardships you had to endure to make it out of kidhood. I know at times it was hard. I so love you guys. You are all remarkable. To my older brother John, to this day you inspire me—I respect you. Thank you for being there. To my childhood friends Danny, Evans, Sharon, we made it out alive and look what God did. So cool.

To John A., my sponsor and fishing partner, thank you.

To my band of brothers from the bunkhouse and base-camp, you guys are important to me. Life is just better with you men. Thank you. Joe Don Flack, Ricky Magee, Donny Discoe, thank you guys for riding shotgun with me on all these crazy, dusty, rocky trails. You guys are my solids.

To Gary Mobley, who has given of his land and resources without hesitation, your crown will be full of jewels brother. More kids have been baptized in your ole deer pond than in most churches! Jesus is proud of you.

To my KOZ Board of Directors — Tom Ball, Alan McGraw, Jimmy Gregory, Joe Don Mayes, Joe Cabela, Trey Webb, Dennis Annabelli, Buck VanTrease, and Steve Hall — who have stood with me through all the seasons that have come and gone, it is a rare thing for a man to have so many good men as friends and confidants. I am blessed. Thanks for believing in and supporting me and KOZ. Because of you, generations are being changed for eternity.

To John Eldredge, Morgan Snyder, Robert Lewis, Tim Clinton, and Stephen Kendrick, you didn't have to be there but you were. Your work for Jesus inspires me to fight for His place in my heart and others'. You are good friends.

To all the KOZ boys, and the KOZ Pinks along the trail, you are a gift from God to me. You have made my life an incredible, beautiful adventure. Remember, Do Hard Things. I love you all.

To the KOZ Team of HTL's, your wives, your pastors, you guys are truly God's KOZ soldiers in the fields of the fatherless. Stand firm. Know that what you are doing matters. You may not see it all here on earth, but my-oh-my when you reach Heaven the crowds will roar. #KOZStrong

Years ago, before I really knew Jesus, a man named Zig Ziglar wrote inside my bible his name and one thing that I want to share with everyone. Romans 10:9, "If you declare with your mouth, 'Jesus is Lord,' and believe in your heart that God raised him from the dead, you will be saved."

For information on Kids Outdoor Zone
go to the website **KidsOutdoorZone.com.**

Social Media: **KidsOutdoorZone | @KidsOutdoorZone |
#KidsOutdoorZone | #KOZStrong**

Made in the USA
Columbia, SC
16 July 2021